Enduring
Wisdom

Lessons from Indiana's Championship
High School Cross Country Coaches

Derek and Gwen Leininger

Original cover photo by Dave Takayoshi, Line 11 Documentary
Photography, www.line11.com
Cover design and photo editing by Gwendolyn Leininger

Derek Leininger
Gwendolyn Leininger
Enduring Wisdom: Lessons from Indiana's Championship High
School Cross Country Coaches

ISBN-13: 978-1545577004
ISBN-10: 1545577005

First published in the United States of America

FIRST EDITION

Contents

Dedicated to all Indiana high school cross country coaches, past and present, whose legacy is evident in the lives of the athletes you coached.

Acknowledgments

This book is the product of collaboration and insight from many people.

To the coaches featured in this book, thank you for your time, your patience, and your willingness to share, as well as your incalculable contributions to high school cross country in Indiana. You have made a difference.

To Rick Weinheimer, Scott Lidskin, Matt Ingalls, Colin Altevogt, and Brad Peterson, thank you for your careful editing and your thoughtful suggestions.

To Dave Takayoshi and Line 11 Documentary Photography, whose photo we adapted to create our cover, thank you for capturing the moments in our sport with your art.

To our family and friends, thank you for your support and encouragement. And especially to Georgia, this book's number one fan, thank you for your enthusiasm, your charming cover art ideas, and your unwavering belief in us.

Look to the heights that are worth your attaining
Keep your feet firm in the path to the goal.
Toward noble deeds every effort be straining.
Worthy ambition is food for the soul!

-Paul Laurence Dunbar

Introduction

Indiana high school cross country boasts a history rich with achievement. But it is facing a challenge that has gone largely unrecognized: an exodus of a generation of remarkable coaches in our sport. As of June 2016, ten of the last twelve state championship coaches in Indiana boys' cross country had retired from coaching or had moved on to coaching out of state or at the collegiate level. Girls' cross country faces a similar lack of experienced championship coaches. As we enter the 2017 cross country season, only one active girls' head coach in Indiana (Scott Lidskin) has ever won a team state championship.

The collective retirement of so many great coaches is more than simply a normal cycling of leadership. Our running community is facing all at once the loss of decades upon decades of coaching experience and knowledge. What a travesty it would be if all that wisdom disappeared without being gathered and recorded. That is where the idea for this book was born. We decided to start interviewing coaches who had reached the highest level of success and find out what made each of them so successful.

The landscape of high school athletics is constantly changing, and this book is our attempt to capture a moment in the history of Indiana distance running. We wanted to pay tribute to those who have influenced the sport and record a portion of the wisdom they gained from experience. Not every coach in this book is on the brink of retirement, but together this group embodies Indiana's tradition of excellence in high school cross country and track and field.

The Selection Process

Our goal was to create a case study group composed of 15-20 coaches. We hoped to find coaches that represented geographic diversity throughout the state, coaches of both boys' and girls' teams, and coaches from different eras (as far back as we could go) that have made Indiana distance running what it is today.

In choosing whom to interview, we created a set of criteria and assigned point values for various coaching accomplishments. These point values helped us narrow our search:

- 2 points – head coach of cross country team state title
- 1 point – head coach of cross country team state runner-up
- 1 point – distance coach of 4x800-meter relay state title
- 1 point – for each individual state cross country champion

Any coach with a total of 4 points or more, or with two individual champions, was invited to take part. We realize that our criteria eliminated a number of exceptional coaches that we could have included in this project. Quite simply, we had to narrow our group to a manageable size for research purposes. The above criteria helped us create the 19-person focus group that we interviewed throughout this project. These coaches represent and epitomize the wisdom of the many influential coaches we were unable to include.

Voice of the Book

The pages that follow are a compilation of information and reflections that form one narrative.

The true voice of this book belongs to the coaches. At times they showed incredible consistency in their responses across a topic; other times their messages differed greatly. When they were consistent, we generalized and made strong, definitive claims. When they differed, we tried to explore the complexity of their positions. We have not attempted to remain stoic reporters of the bare facts, but instead we have made many observations and editorialized while staying true to the words and spirit of those we interviewed. We have even included stories or concepts that don't seem to be about running at all but that provide an interesting frame for understanding the wisdom of these coaches. Even though the words were ours, we worked diligently to make sure the voice belonged to our 19 championship coaches.

In the second half of the book we have included several chapters about distance training. We purposely stayed away from being overly scientific and technical in writing those chapters. There are many excellent technical books on training distance runners, written by authors and researchers with far better exercise science credentials than we possess. We felt that readers of this book would benefit more if we were to present the coaches' training just as they explained it. In the training chapters, you will read authentic accounts of how our coaches applied training theory in a real setting. We hope that authenticity is helpful for the reader.

About the Authors

Derek Leininger is the original creator and current co-owner of IndianaRunner.com. Indiana Runner has been covering Indiana high school cross country and track and field since June 2000, when

Derek was a sophomore runner for Columbia City High School, where he was All-State in the 800-meter run. Derek's years of experience with Indiana Runner and his involvement with the Indiana Association of Track and Cross Country Coaches (IATCCC) have given him unique insight and connections with some of the best cross country coaches in the state, which helped turn the idea of this book into a reality.

Gwen Leininger is a professional writer, focusing primarily on topics related to public education. She was an Indiana high school All-State cross country runner at Rushville Consolidated High School and a cross country and track DIII All-American and school record holder at Anderson University.

Derek and Gwen are married, and they coached high school cross country and track & field together over the course of thirteen years, including Derek's ten years as the head cross country coach at Snider High School in Fort Wayne, IN. During their tenure, Snider's cross country teams won four conference titles and qualified for three state finals. Snider also won the 2010 state title in the boys' 4x400-meter relay and state runner-up finishes in 2010 and 2011 in the boys' 4x800-meter relay. The team also earned three Hoosier State Relays (HSR) indoor titles in the boys' 4x800. Snider's 2012 4x800-meter relay team still holds the all-time Indiana indoor state record.

Derek and Gwen have retired from coaching to pursue other professional interests, but their hearts are still strongly connected to high school cross country and track & field in the state of Indiana.

Chapter 1: The Coaches

Colin Altevogt

Colin Altevogt is the head boys' cross country coach and assistant boys' track & field coach at Carmel HS. Altevogt has ten years of coaching experience dating back to his college years as an assistant coach at Columbus North HS under Hall of Fame coach Rick Weinheimer. He has been on coaching staffs for five state championship teams in cross country and two in track & field. He holds a bachelor's degree from Franklin College and a master's degree from Ball State University in secondary education. He lives in Carmel, IN with his wife, Cathleen.

Erhard Bell

As a full-time physician, Erhard "Doc" Bell has coached boys' and girls' cross country and track & field for twelve years at Carmel HS, Brebeuf HS, and Southport HS. Bell spent five years as boys' head cross country coach at Carmel, where his 2012 and 2013 teams were state champions. He coached two individual 1600-meter state champions, a boys' 4x800-meter relay state championship and multiple All-State runners and relays. He was an All-State runner on the 1975 Southport HS state champion cross country team and he remains the only person in Indiana history to be both an athlete on an Indiana state championship team and the head coach of a state championship team.

Joe Brooks

Joe Brooks began coaching in 1979 and from 1983 to 2011 he was the head boys' cross country coach at Warren Central HS. In cross country his teams won 11 sectional, 6 regional, 2 semi-state, and 2 state championships. As a track & field assistant coach (distance), Brooks was part of 4 state track & field team championships. In 2006, he coached the #4 all-time Indiana 4x1600-meter relay team (17:29) and #10 all-time 4x800-meter relay team (7:44). In 2007, his distance medley relay ran 10:18 for # 8 all-time. He coached two individual state champions: Brad Griggs (1995 800m) and DeSean Turner (2006 XC, 2007 1600m).

Karen DeVries

Karen DeVries coached girls' cross country as head coach from 1987 to 2011 and assistant (distance) track & field coach from 1988 to 2012 at Valparaiso HS. During her career, DeVries' team qualified for the state cross country meet 22 out of 25 years. Her 1999 team won the state cross country championship, which began an eight-year streak of winning the state meet five times and finishing runner-up three times. In track she coached a state champion 4x800-meter relay team (1997), two 1600-meter run individual state champions (1991, 2006) and two 3200-meter run individual state champions (1991, 2009). She was a two-time ICGSA coach of the year, was inducted into Wadsworth HS Hall of Fame in 2006, the IATCCC Hall of Fame in 2012, and the Medina County Hall of Fame in 2015.

Mark Ellington

Mark Ellington coached boys' track & field at Clay Middle School in Carmel, IN from 1999 to 2010, boys' and girls' cross country at Clay MS from 2001 to 2008, and served as the girls' cross country head coach at Carmel HS from 2009 to 2016. During Ellington's high school coaching career, his teams qualified for the state finals 8 times, earning one state runner-up and seven consecutive state titles (a state record). These teams also competed in Nike Cross Nationals (NXN) and qualified for the finals seven consecutive times (2010-2016). They won the NXR Midwest team title five times (2011-2014, 2016) and were runners up once (2010). Their seven appearances at NXN all resulted in top-8 team finishes (3rd twice, 4th twice, 5th, 7th, and 8th).

Josh Fletcher

Josh Fletcher coached boys' cross country for thirteen years and girls' track & field for fifteen years at Northridge HS. Since 2014, Fletcher has been coaching girls' track & field at Penn HS with one year as girls' cross country head coach. During his career he has coached eight top-10 team finishes at the state cross country finals with a state championship in 2004. In track & field he coached two 4x800-meter relay state championships and an 800-meter run individual state champion. His fastest girls' 4x800-meter relay team (9:01) ranks #4 in Indiana history. In the 3200-meter run, he has coached five different female runners under 11:03. He has coached a total of 27 All-State athletes in cross country and track.

Steve Kearney

Steve Kearney has coached for 47 years: cross country and track and field at Chesterton HS as well as with the Calumet Region Striders and adult distance runners. As a head cross country coach, Kearney's teams qualified for the state meet ten times and placed in the top 10 seven times. Three of his track and field teams placed in the top 5 at the state meet, and he coached three state record-breaking girls' 4x800-meter relay teams in 2003, 2004, and 2006. His fastest girls' 4x800-meter relay team (9:03) ranks #6 all-time in Indiana history, and his fastest girls' distance medley relay team (12:24) ranks #10 all-time.

Eric Kellison

Eric Kellison started coaching in 1990, and from 1992 to 2012 he served as the head boys' cross country coach and assistant boys' track & field coach (distance) at Franklin Central HS. From 1999 to 2002 Kellison also served as head girls' cross country coach. His boys' cross country teams earned eight top-10 state meet finishes, with one team state title and two team state runner-up finishes. In four years of coaching girls' cross country, his teams earned three top-10 finishes. He coached 18 All-State cross country runners and two IHSAA Mental Attitude Award winners. In track he coached 11 All-State individuals (one state champion) and 5 All-State 4x800-meter relay teams (one state champion). He was the youngest coach ever to be inducted into the IATCCC Hall of Fame at 43 years young.

Chuck Koeppen

Chuck Koeppen was born and raised in Valparaiso, IN, in a large, hard-working family. He coached at Daleville HS from 1968 to '69, Wapahani HS from 1969 to '72, and Carmel HS from 1972 to 2008. At Carmel, Koeppen's boys' cross country teams won 11 state titles and 9 runner-up finishes. His girls' cross country teams won 11 state titles, 6 state runner-up finishes, and two individual state champions. In boys' track & field, he was the head coach of the 2000 state team champions. He also coached three boys' 4x800-meter relay team champions and three individual track state champions, one each in the boys' 800, 1600 and 3200. He was the 1982 national high school cross country coach of the year and the 2000 national high school track & field coach of the year. In 2013 he was inducted into the NFHS Hall of Fame. He has served for 36 years as the director of the All Star Cross Country Camp. He retired from coaching at Carmel in 2008 and currently serves as the head coach of men's cross country and track and field at IUPUI. He is married to his wife Cathie, and they have four children—Carrie, Cherie, Christie and Charlie—and seven grandchildren.

Steve Lewark

Steve Lewark coached boys' and girls' cross country and track and field for 22 years from 1995 to 2016. Lewark spent 21 years as the head boys' cross country coach, 17 years as the head girls' cross country coach, and 22 years as an assistant track and field coach at West Lafayette HS. During his career he coached 21 state-qualifying cross country teams, including 9 podium (top-5) finishes and the 2014 boys state championship. He also coached five state 4x800-meter relay state champions, three individual state champions, and four IHSAA Mental Attitude Award winners. His girls' 4x800, 4x1600 and DMR rank #2 in Indiana history, and his boys' 4x1600 and DMR rank #1 and #2 in Indiana history.

Scott Lidskin

Scott Lidskin began his running career in 1989 as a freshman at Glenbrook South HS in Illinois. Lidskin placed runner up in the Illinois high school cross country state finals his senior year and went on to earn four team MVP awards as Butler University's top runner, and he holds a PR of 13:59 for 5000 meters. He began his coaching career in 1996 at Westfield HS and has coached the girls' cross country team there for 19 years. During that time he coached four IHSAA girls' state championship cross country teams (1998, 2005, 2006, 2007), one state runner-up team (2004), and eleven top-10 team finishes. Additionally, he has coached two girls' 4x800-meter relay state championship teams in track.

Barrie Peterson

Barrie Peterson began his coaching career in 1966 at Central HS in Fort Wayne, IN. Peterson spent most of his career as the head boys' cross country coach at Northrop HS. While at Northrop, his teams earned 21 conference, 17 sectional, 17 regional and 4 semi-state team championships. His teams qualified for 21 state finals in cross country, earning fifteen top-10 finishes, including four team runner-up finishes. He coached 20 All-State cross country athletes and 2 IHSAA Mental Attitude Award winners. As head track and field coach at Northrop, he coached nine top-10 state meet finishes, including the 1997 team state champions. He coached 7 individual state champions and 8 runners-up in track and 2 IHSAA Mental Attitude Award winners.

Brad Peterson

Brad Peterson coached boys' and girls' cross country and track and field for ten years in Indiana, from 1996 to 2006, and 2013 to 2015. Peterson coached from 1997 to 1999 at Northrop HS and from 1999 to 2006 at Concordia Lutheran HS. During those years, his cross country teams qualified for the state meet every year and earned eight top-10 finishes. He coached 12 different individual state champions between cross country and track. Many of his athletes are still listed in the top 10 all-time in Indiana in their event. He coached 4 different teams to state runner-up finishes, highlighted by an 81-point performance in 2004 with Concordia girls' track and field.

Mike Prow

Mike Prow began coaching in 1981 at Belzer Middle School in Lawrence Township. From 1990 to 2014 he served as the boys' head cross country coach and assistant track & field coach at Valparaiso HS. During that time Prow coached 21 state-qualifying cross country teams, including sixteen top-10 team finishes, twelve podium (top-5) teams, a state runner-up team in 2005, and two state championship teams (1997, 2000). He coached eleven different All-State individuals in cross country. He currently lives in Sedona, AZ, where he teaches and coaches high school cross country.

Zach Raber

Zach Raber coached boys' and girls' cross country and track and field at Carroll HS from 2002 to 2013. While at Carroll, Raber's boys' teams earned two runner-up state meet finishes. He coached the girls' teams to 11 consecutive sectional and regional titles. His girls' teams also won four semi-state titles and three top-5 finishes at the state finals. Individually, he coached 25 All-State individuals between track and cross country, including three state champions. On the national level, he coached 10 individual All-Americans. In 2013 his boys' 4x800-meter relay team won the New Balance National Outdoor Championship after earning All-American status the previous season. He is currently the men's and women's head cross country coach at Trine University.

Sam Rasmussen

Sam Rasmussen retired in 2011 after 40 years in education as a teacher, coach, and athletic director—all but one of those years at Valparaiso HS. He taught science at Valparaiso, where he coached cross country from 1974 to 1975 and then from 1984 to 1988. He coached track and field from 1975 to 1986, with an undefeated streak in the regular seasons from 1981 to 1983, compiling 80 consecutive wins, and going undefeated again in 1985. His 1985 and 1986 boys' cross country teams won team state titles, and he was named Indiana boys' cross country coach of the year both years. He also was chosen Indiana track and field coach of the year twice. In retirement he served three years as executive director of the Indiana Interscholastic Athletic Administrators Association (IIAAA). Rasmussen served for several years as the summer program director at Onseyawa Handicapped Children Camp and the developer and director of Camp Pocohachi Handicapped Children Camp.

Tim Ray

Tim Ray is currently the head boys' cross country coach and assistant track and field coach at Chesterton HS. Ray has been the head cross country coach for 15 years and assistant track coach (distance) for 17 years. Tim has coached 11 state cross country qualifying teams, including the state runners-up in 2009. He has coached numerous individual All-State cross country runners. In track he coached the 2014 state champion 4x800-meter relay team, after they finished as state runners-up the year before. He has also coached 11 state-qualifying 4x800-meter relay teams with 8 top-10 finishes and multiple individual and relay state medalists. His fastest 4x800-meter relay team (7:43) ranks #8 all-time in Indiana.

Rick Stover

Rick Stover began his coaching career in 1975 at Westlane Junior High. He spent most of his career at North Central HS in Indianapolis, where he coached from 1985 to 2012. During Stover's tenure at North Central, his boys' cross country teams earned 8 podium finishes. He coached 16 individual All-State runners, including two individual state cross country champions (Bart Phariss and Futsum Zienasellassie). As head boys' track and field coach, his teams were state runners-up twice, and he coached three individual state champions and three state championship relay teams. Under his coaching, Futsum Zienasellassie ran

12

8:47 for 3200 meters, which is the fastest time in Indiana history.

Rick Weinheimer

Rick Weinheimer has coached the Columbus North HS boys' cross country team since 1979 and girls' cross country team since they started the program in 1981. Weinheimer's 52 state-finalist teams have included 28 podium (top-5) finishes, including 6 team state championships and 5 team state runners-up. Those teams have won 44 conference titles and over 120 tournament championships. Four teams finished the season in the top 10 in the nation. Having coached 63 All-State cross country individuals and 35 track All-State runners, he has been named Indiana coach of the year 10 times, has been a nominee for national coach of the year four times, and was inducted into the IATCCC Hall of Fame in 2004.

Enduring Wisdom

Chapter 2: The Personality of a Great Coach

"I am a fighter and a competitor and someone who does not give up easily ... I never gave up on my team."
- Karen DeVries

We have introduced the coaches and their major accomplishments, but we wondered if there was something deeper about their personalities that helped make them successful. We hoped to identify character traits they had in common. Would we find trends and patterns in the way great coaches think, interact with people, and run their programs? To begin this project, we prescribed a Myers-Briggs personality test for each coach. The test provided a fun way to learn more about our coaches, but mostly it functioned as a lens through which we saw more general personality traits: the great coaches were positive and engaging, tuned in and flexible, meticulous and traditional, idealistic and selfless.

The test assigned each coach a four-letter typology measuring four different "functions" or traits. Here is a simplified explanation of the Myers-Briggs Typology Indicator, which comes from Carl Jung's theory of psychological types. (If you want a more in-depth explanation or to take your own Myers-Briggs test, check out the website we used for this research, 16personalities.com.)

PERSONALITY TEST RESULTS

Colin Altevogt	I	S	F	J
Erhard Bell	E	S	F	J
Joe Brooks	E	S	F	J
Karen DeVries	I	N	F	J
Mark Ellington	E	S	F	J
Josh Fletcher	E	S	F	J
Steve Kearney	I	S	F	P
Eric Kellison	E	S	F	J
Chuck Koeppen	E	S	F	J
Steve Lewark	I	S	F	J
Scott Lidskin	I	S	T	J
Barrie Peterson	E	S	F	J
Brad Peterson	E	S	F	J
Michael Prow	E	S	F	J
Zach Raber	I	N	F	J
Sam Rasmussen	I	S	F	J
Tim Ray	I	N	F	P
Rick Stover	I	S	F	J
Rick Weinheimer	I	S	F	J

Four Letter Possibilities:

E or I - (E)xtravert or (I)ntrovert - *Does the person get energy from the external world or the internal? This affects the way the following functions play out.*
S or N - (S)ensing or I(N)tuition - *Does the person perceive the world more through conscious sensing or through unconscious instinct?*
T or F - (T)hinking or (F)eeling - *Does the person make judgments more through active, directed thought, or a subjective feeling that something should be accepted or rejected?*
J or P - (J)udging or (P)erceiving - *Which of the two previous functions (Perceiving is the S/N function and Judging is the T/F function) is dominant?*

Positive and Engaging

When we began this project, we hypothesized that most coaches would be extraverts, since their job requires that they lead people. Our culture commonly assumes that extraverts are better leaders than introverts. "In a 2006 survey, 65% of senior corporate executives viewed introversion as a barrier to leadership, and other studies have shown that highly extroverted U.S. presidents are perceived as more effective" (Grant, 2010). A full 96 percent of leaders and managers report being extraverted (Grant, 2014), so we figured the same might hold true for coaches.

It turns out we were wrong. Out of the 19 coaches in our group, 9 of them (47%) reported being extraverts and 10 of them (53%) reported being introverts. This information surprised us at first glance. When we dug a little deeper into the data, we learned that extraverts and introverts may approach leadership differently, but they can be equally effective.

Perhaps results would differ in other sports, but the idea that introversion is a barrier to success was certainly not true in our study of cross country coaches. Far more important was that the coaches remain positive and engaging, whatever their personality.

Positive interactions come naturally to Mark Ellington, an extravert who calls himself a consensus builder. "I can engage most anyone in a positive manner. Whether it's an athlete, a parent, fellow coaches, administrators, I seem to be able to connect with them," he told us. Chuck Koeppen, another extravert, says a great coach is a "tremendous diplomat," referencing the need for a head coach to balance numerous types of relationships. These two coaches had unparalleled success, and their personalities fit our expected mold of extraverted leadership and connecting with people.

The introverts in our group are equally focused on others, emphasizing positive relationships just as much as the extraverts. Introvert Scott Lidskin of Westfield says he internalized the value of strong communication from his parents, and he tries to be "assertive in a compassionate way." Sam Rasmussen, an introvert, mentioned enthusiasm more than once, while another introvert, Karen DeVries, told us that a great coach has to be optimistic and encouraging, a "cheerer in all of life." Introvert Steve Kearney talked about getting "excited about athletic performance from emerging young people." Rick Weinheimer is another who doesn't let introversion get in the way of positive leadership: "I often have to push myself when I am in leadership roles. It comes naturally in some ways, and in some ways I would prefer to blend in." Whether or not they are naturally charismatic, all of our coaches talked about investing in the people around them. In our research, being an extravert or an introvert made no real difference in a coach's ability to succeed at the highest level, so long as the coach engaged people in a positive way.

Tuned In and Flexible

The personality study got more interesting as we looked at personality functions beyond introversion and extraversion. Rick Weinheimer's sometime desire to "blend in" is not unusual for someone with his personality type. He's an ISFJ, along with Colin Altevogt, Sam Rasmussen, Rick Stover and Steve Lewark. According to 16Personalities, ISFJs are often a little uncomfortable in the spotlight. Yet they're typically good with people because they tend to see the best in others and are aware of other people's feelings. They aren't always outgoing, but ISFJs develop people skills with a genuinely altruistic purpose. They're likely to be tuned in to others.

Weinheimer described a sixth sense that he has developed in working with young people. "Sometimes I have an intuitive feeling that something is wrong with certain runners. Maybe it's subconsciously interpreting body language or reactions. But I am almost always right when I think something is wrong." Brad Peterson chose the word "observant" to describe the personality of a great coach. He believes that an ability to notice details and tune in to a runner's unspoken needs is what allows a great coach to make necessary day-to-day adjustments. "For example, Brett Tipton may have had a prescribed 10x400 with 60-second rest with a goal time of 62 seconds. However, he may have looked flat throughout, so I would alter the workout to 8 or 9x400 and perhaps increase rest to 90 seconds on the latter ones." Peterson does this all the time, with workouts rarely ever going as planned. If Peterson has 15 kids doing 400 repeats, he says only about ⅓ of them usually do the exact prescribed workout. "You have to read every single kid and how they are feeling physically, but also personally how they are doing in life. Many factors go into being an observant and effective coach. There are people that just have that feel, and that is what makes them great."

Steve Lewark didn't begin coaching until the age of 48, after many years as an accountant. His career in accounting helped him learn to work calmly and flexibly with many different kinds of people. Likewise, Zach Raber calls training "a fluid process [that] isn't the same for everyone," and he's always honing his intuitive interpersonal skills, learning "when to put your arm around [the athletes] and talk them up or ... when to really get after them." These coaches tune in and adjust to unspoken needs.

Perhaps some people are naturally more tuned in than others, but that doesn't mean a coach can't intentionally cultivate this trait. Rick Stover realized after his third year coaching at North Central that he was "breaking" too many runners. "I realized at that time that I was not paying enough attention to how my runners were handling the workouts. I was not flexible on the quantities of intervals and mileage," he said. So Stover borrowed from his experience as a math teacher. He started using the term "x" as a stand-in for the quantity in a workout. When athletes asked how many 400s they were doing, Stover would reply, "x." He would have a number in mind, but when he felt that they had had enough, he would tell them they had reached "x"; and when they seemed able to handle more than his original plan, using "x" allowed him to keep them going. "That also took care of those who would save for that last interval and blitz it while they were slacking for most of the first part of the workout."

Tuning in and constantly adjusting the plan is important to Steve Kearney too. Kearney is an ISFP, a personality type that tends to be charming and willing to try new things. So we thought it was fitting that, when asked what aspects of his personality served him well as a coach, Kearney's first answer was "being flexible." He said that he usually approaches coaching as a science, but then finishes it as an art, which to him means being "flexible, adaptable, and creative."

Meticulous and Traditional

Fifteen of our coaches—a whopping 74%—are part of a group nicknamed "sentinels" by Myers-Briggs analysts, which includes any "_S_J" type. This high number surprised us, considering this type makes up only 38% of the general population. But when we learned more about "sentinels," we weren't so surprised. They are supposed to be good in administrative roles: they're known for craving order and tradition, upholding community values, being meticulous and hardworking. So it's not particularly surprising to see them in a coaching role, especially the many extraverted ESFJs, who are typically well-liked and sociable.

Barrie Peterson pointed to a hard work ethic, "stick-to-itiveness," and punctuality as some of the personality traits that have served him well, and several coaches, including Scott Lidskin, lauded the importance of being organized. Nearly every coach we talked with meticulously keeps records of workout and race results, logging hours of planning outside of practice each week. Lidskin's ISTJ personality type is known for being logical, detail-oriented, hard-working, devoted to integrity, and reliable—qualities that earn them respect and make them beloved leaders.

Idealistic and Selfless

Karen DeVries, Zach Raber, and Tim Ray are classified as "diplomats" based on their four-letter types. These are the idealists of the group. They're all introverts, but their passion for creating something beautiful—a team of individuals pushing their limits for the sake of the group—makes them magnetic interpersonal leaders. DeVries displays her idealism in the emphasis she places on team camaraderie, a value she picked up from her own high school coach. "When you train, you are training for your teammate, and when you toe the line to race, you are toeing that line for your teammate. And each person on that team competing should be able to look over at their teammate standing next to them and say, 'I will run hard for you today because I know you prepared yourself to run hard for me.'" This is the kind of passionate speech that's been delivered in locker rooms for generations, regardless of a coach's personality type, and we're confident that many of the coaches in this book would agree with that sentiment. But this speech is also a clue to the INFJ personality type shared by DeVries and Raber. INFJs are very rare, only 1% of the population, because while they are idealists, they are also unfailingly practical. These are the dreamers who, having built castles in the air, have no trouble proceeding to put foundations under them. DeVries' earnest belief that teammates should train and race for each other isn't just about warm feelings of support and unity; it is also a call to pragmatic, daily, selfless action. Idealism plus practicality.

Tim Ray, our only INFP, talked to us about the importance of relational versatility; to him, the art of coaching means taking a wide range of runners, all with different backgrounds and commitment levels, and motivating them to perform at "levels that they may not consider themselves worthy of." The selflessness in his statement is almost palpable, and it's clear that his coaching is athlete-centered. He concentrates most of his time on personalizing his coaching because, as he puts it, "There is no handbook to be laid out for working with these different student athletes."

A selfless focus on others has also served Mark Ellington as a coach. It is a trait we noticed in him when we asked about how he first got into coaching. He was a senior runner at Carmel HS, where the team was so large and talented that he knew he wouldn't run varsity—there were dozens of athletes beating his times (he ran 4:50 for 1600 and 10:10 for 3200). So when Coach Kevin Karns asked him if he'd be interested in forgoing his own senior track season to help coach the freshmen, Ellington said yes. (At that time, Carmel's ninth grade was part of the middle school and thus was coached separately, except for those few talented enough to join the varsity team.) He had known he would not continue a serious running career after high school, and his career goal was to become a teacher and coach, so Ellington jumped at the opportunity. "I liked the idea that I might be able to contribute to the team," he said. And so Mark Ellington began his coaching career. He didn't have disciplinary control, but he guided athletes and had some say in the making of the lineups.

When we heard this story, we were struck with Ellington's willingness to give up his own senior track season in order to help younger athletes. But he told us, "I didn't feel like I was sacrificing much in not being on the track team that season. I had a great experience. It was a complete honor. Especially in that [Coach Karns] trusted what I had learned through high school and believed I could transfer my experience to a group of freshmen to make them better and help make their team competitive." It speaks to Ellington's values that he found more gain in building up others than in focusing on himself. In his words, "You can really only collect so much for yourself in this life. In the end, it gets a little boring. Try investing in others and you develop a real sense of purpose in what you do daily. I'm not perfect in the execution. I have to be brought back from time to time, but really it's been true my whole life."

Chapter 3: Success Takes Time

"The tipping point for me came in about 1999,
when I decided to concentrate less on the
achievements and more on the development of
athletes, both as runners and as people."
- Rick Weinheimer

Success takes time, even for the best of the best. Our coaches have won a combined 56 team state championships in cross country, not to mention individual champions, podium team finishes, and accomplishments in track and field. The coaches on this list have won 28 of the past 40 boys' team titles and 27 of the past 35 titles on the girls' side. It would be easy to assume that success came fairly quickly for coaches such as these, but it did not.

Our coaches average 25 years of coaching experience. On average, they took 11 years to win a state title. Many did not win state until almost halfway through their careers! Four of our coaches did not win a state championship until after 20 years of coaching! For Steve Lewark it took 20 years; for Joe Brooks, 22; for Rick Weinheimer, 24; and for Barrie Peterson it took 30 years. Success, at the very highest level, rarely comes quickly.

Success is a Tsunami

Writer Malcolm Gladwell has popularized the research of a psychologist named K. Anders Ericsson, who said it takes 10,000 hours of deliberate practice for even the most talented people to become world-class (Ericsson, Krampe, & Tesch-Römer, 1993) (Gladwell, 2008). Even when success seems to come like a quick tidal wave, a closer look shows the energy building beneath the surface. A tsunami, for example, can travel at 500 miles per hour across an ocean and go unnoticed by sailors at the surface until it approaches the shore. Its massive amount of energy travels through the deep water, sometimes only showing surface waves that are less than a foot high. But as it enters shallower water, the energy has nowhere to go but up, and it "shoals" into waves that suddenly increase in height (Science Learning Hub, 2011). The ocean's powerful rise comes seemingly out of nowhere. A steady rise and fall suddenly builds up into something spectacular (National Geographic News, 2007).

That is precisely what happened for Rick Weinheimer. He began coaching cross country at Columbus North HS in 1979. Over the next 20 years he did very well, with his teams qualifying for the state meet yearly. His girls' teams in particular finished in the top five several times, and were state runners-up in 1986. But Weinheimer had never won that elusive state title. That didn't happen until 2001, and when it did, his program seemed to have built an unstoppable momentum, winning six titles (five boys' and one girls') over his final fifteen years of coaching.

So what exactly happened to buoy Weinheimer from good to great, to make his a face that would go on the Mount Rushmore of Indiana high school cross country? In 1999, Weinheimer had an epiphany: "I decided to concentrate less on the achievements and more on the development of athletes, both as runners and as people. The longer I've coached, the more I've realized that the actual skills for the sport are not particularly valuable assets for life. The lifelong valuable benefits of the sport are more of the other skills: work ethic, positive attitude, perspective, organization, every day dedication, leadership, contributing to a group, etc. I feel driven to make a difference in people's lives, so to truly make a difference I needed to spend more purposeful attention

26

on teaching and practicing those lifelong skills, not just mentioning them in a 'Knute Rockne' speech, but paying specific attention by teaching them thoroughly and giving runners feedback as they practice them. The tipping point came when I began concentrating on those skills with each runner Every Day."

Weinheimer realized that his dream of a state title was, to some degree, outside of his control, but that the truly valuable achievements for his athletes could be realized if he focused on excellence "Every Day." For more on this Every Day approach, we highly recommend Weinheimer's book, *Move Your Chair*.

Culture is the Tipping Point

A tipping point—that moment when the wave's energy reaches a threshold and rises dramatically into a formidable force—was evident for a majority of the coaches we interviewed. For most of them, the tipping point was a change in team culture. Tim Ray recalls a change in expectations, "the start of changing the culture of running at Chesterton." After this culture change, his boys would qualify for the state meet the next twelve consecutive years (2000-2011), including a state runner-up finish in 2009.

Josh Fletcher's alma mater, Northridge, had only qualified for the state meet one time: his senior year. So when he returned to coach there, his storied success as an athlete helped the runners believe in his training and gave them a common vision and a desire to work together toward it. Within three years, they would bring their school to the state meet, and keep going back for nine consecutive years, even winning a state title in 2004.

For Joe Brooks, a culture change began in 1999 when, after winning semi-state for the first time, the athletes were disappointed with a seventh-place finish at state. After that disappointment, more runners bought into the idea that they needed to train year-round. "Instead of a few runners running 500 miles in the summer we had 10 to 12. We got on the podium for the first time the following year by placing 5th in the 2000 State Meet." Five years later, motivated further by another disappointment in 2004, the team's ethos of hard work came to fruition, so that they knew they truly belonged in the state meet. "The 2005 season was a dream season. We went undefeated and our team qualified for the Nike Team Nationals in Portland, Oregon where we placed 14th."

Zach Raber of Carroll also acknowledged the importance of a culture change, noting that "the greatest tipping point for me was the athletes' finally buying into what we were doing 100%." These stories of success all fit a narrative arc of a team of athletes beginning to buy into what their coach was selling. The specifics of training philosophy and strategy were of secondary importance. What really mattered was whether the athletes believed in it. With every interview we heard the same message: when athletes began to "buy in," recognizing the value of working hard toward their team's shared purpose and setting high expectations for themselves, results quickly followed.

We see one such example in the 1998 Northrop boys' middle-distance team. Their head track coach, Hall of Famer Barrie Peterson, brought his son Brad onto the coaching staff. One hallmark of a great leader is the ability to recognize the strengths of others and the willingness to bring them in, even if it means sharing the spotlight. Barrie calls Brad "the real expert on 800 training," and so he handed Brad the reigns for training the middle-distance boys. Barrie's wisdom in delegating responsibility was well-timed; 1998 happened to be the junior year of a tall, athletic blonde kid named Brett Tipton. Tipton and the younger Peterson just "clicked," and Tipton was willing to work hard and listen. A coaching change can throw off a group of runners, and Brad had big shoes to fill. But when the junior surprised much of Indiana by winning the state title in the 1600 in 4:14, it became obvious to the rest of the team that they could trust this new coach the way they trusted his father. "I think I will always owe a lot of my success as a coach to Brett Tipton. I was lucky enough to coach him, but also lucky enough that he trusted me and got everyone else around him to trust in me," Brad said. Tipton went on to defend his 1600 state title as a senior, and guess who was the state runner-up? His teammate, Nathan Peffley. That year Northrop's 4x800 team also placed sixth without Tipton or Peffley on the relay. Northrop's entire middle-distance team had quickly become a state powerhouse. Tipton went on to split 1:49 in the 4x800 at Nationals and won the indoor national 800-meter run title, and Brad went on to coach eleven more individual or relay state champions. Without Brad's expertise, Tipton may not have been a state champion. Without Tipton's trust, Brad's rise to the ranks of top coaches may have taken much longer. The tipping point was the intersection of two people who each needed the other's strengths and were given the chance to work together.

The Timing of the Culture Change

In some cases, an athlete like Brett Tipton was instrumental in changing that culture. In other cases, an athlete benefits from an already changing team culture and uses his or her own energy to accelerate it, keeping the wave crashing ever higher. Coach Eric

Kellison saw a tipping point occur right before three-time state cross country champion Aaron Fisher arrived at Franklin Central HS in 1997. Franklin Central had never qualified for the state meet, but starting with Fisher's sophomore year, Kellison's boys qualified for eight of the next eleven state finals and won one state title (1998) and two runner-up finishes (1999 and 2006). From the outside looking in, you would think Fisher was the primary catalyst to this run of success. His attitude and work ethic were essential to sustaining its momentum, but the real tipping point was a culture change Kellison noticed in the team immediately preceding Fisher's arrival. Kellison had been trying desperately to get kids running in the summer, making phone calls every day, over 100 phone calls in a summer! Then two very dedicated runners, Mark Rode and Matt Sweetman, joined the team as freshmen. They truly loved running and "took no BS from the upperclassmen." Rode and Sweetman worked hard and, Kellison credits them with making their teammates realize "that I was not a screaming fool!" Rode and Sweetman set the table for Fisher's success, and Fisher seemed to recognize the gift he had been given: he took responsibility for continuing the momentum. Kellison stressed that top runners must lead by example, as the hardest workers. "Sometimes I stressed this loudly in private and sometimes in public, but nonetheless the point was taken." So Fisher intentionally perpetuated a positive culture, catapulting his team to great success. By the time he graduated, the culture transformation was complete: although Fisher's teammates didn't make it with him to state his senior year, they placed seventh in state the following year, without him. From that point on, Kellison says, "the guys would do anything I asked."

The Coach as Scientist and Artist

Part of the reason this culture change usually takes so long is that coaching requires study and learning about the body. The coaches generally considered "science" to involve all of the things that are physically happening with each athlete. They mentioned physiology, periodization (peaking at the right time), heart rate, recovery, nutrition, hydration, iron levels, sleep, injury prevention, racing strategy, anatomy, biomechanics, VO2 intervals, anaerobic threshold, tempos, fartlek runs, kinesiology, and injury prevention. Eric Kellison mentioned the importance of documenting and analyzing data from workouts and races. Steve Kearney talked about the importance of studying "the methods of the masters that have gone before." But beyond all this scientific learning, they also consider coaching to be an art. And it takes time to develop as an artist.

In general, art was thought to include motivating athletes, mental preparation and mental training, individualizing your approach for each athlete, your coaching philosophy and team culture, applying the science in your own way, and the ability to adapt your plan. As Tim Ray pointed out, the science of coaching cross country is essentially the same for everyone, but the art of coaching is applying that science in the real world, with a vast number of variables. Dealing with those variables is the art of coaching, and our coaches emphasized its importance. When asked if the "science" or "art" elements were more important, most favored art, with their average estimate being that coaching is 57% art and 43% science. Individually, 12 coaches (63%) said art was more important, 3 coaches (16%) said it was an equal 50-50, and only 4 coaches (21%) said science was more important. Josh Fletcher summed it up: "Any coach can write the best workout, but the way it's implemented is the most important."

However, our question wasn't totally fair, because the art of coaching is inextricable from the science. Leonardo da Vinci became more of a scientist the more he practiced his art, and more of an artist as he studied science. Distance running is like this. As you learn race strategy, you increase both scientific study and your ability to get a feel for when to make a move. As you train your athletes mentally, you call on established brain science while trying to pinpoint a runner's unique psychological hangups. As you manage and prevent injuries, you learn measurable and predictable physiology while also finding ways to tailor the science to the specific needs of the athlete. Colin Altevogt coached Ben Veatch, one of Indiana's all-time great distance runners who repeatedly dealt with injury issues. While Veatch's training plan was grounded in scientific study, Altevogt had to be very creative and adaptive (artistic) with Veatch to keep him healthy and racing at his best, often by reducing his mileage at strategic points during his training.

The science and art of coaching are not two scales to be balanced. They are two supports holding up the same structure. They are not the gas pedal and the brake, where you let up on one as you press down on the other. They are the gas and the clutch, working together. The elite coaches understand the science, but they have also mastered the art of applying that science in an unpredictable world. They understand that there is more than bare mechanical science at work, and they put in the time required to master their art.

Look closely at the science of the runner's body, and you see art. Express it artistically, and you can't help but display the glorious science of the systems working efficiently. This is what Karen DeVries meant when she told us that, to a coach, a strong running form is "something beautiful to look at, and is 'art in motion.'" Coaching is a systematic study of physical performance and improvement, and of methods for putting together the pieces of a successful team. But it is also an expressive application of creative skill and imagination, something that requires a personal touch. It takes so much time to succeed because it requires the slow development of both a scientist and an artist.

Great Leaders are Developed

Success takes time because developing into someone who can change a culture takes time. We asked our 19 coaches if they believe great leaders are born or made, and 18 of them said that great leaders are made. They emphasized the importance of the mentorship, hard work, and patient growth it takes to become a leader, even for someone born with innate leadership potential. As Mike Prow put it, "They don't have a mold" for great leaders. Only one, Josh Fletcher, said that he believes great leaders are born, because of his belief that God creates people with a plan in mind. But elsewhere in his interview he credited the many coaches who mentored him and emphasized the effort of reading coaching books and developing his ideas, so we think it's safe to say all 19 of our legends have embraced, on some level, the notion that leadership potential must be developed to fruition. They all have some unique giftedness for what they do, but none of them has risen to greatness immediately and easily or without help from others. Developing their talent, being willing to grow and listen to the wisdom of others, and working diligently day in and day out, these coaches practice what they preach to their athletes. Perhaps that is one reason their teams have bought in.

Question Posed: "What percentage of coaching is art, and what percentage is science, with the total equaling 100%?"

Coach's Name	Art	Science
Sam Rasmussen	80%	20%
Tim Ray	80%	20%
Barrie Peterson	75%	25%
Michael Prow	75%	25%
Rick Stover	70%	30%
Joe Brooks	65%	35%
Scott Lidskin	65%	35%
Brad Peterson	60%	40%
Chuck Koeppen	60%	40%
Josh Fletcher	60%	40%
Steve Lewark	60%	40%
Zach Raber	60%	40%
Erhard Bell	50%	50%
Karen DeVries	50%	50%
Steve Kearney	50%	50%
Eric Kellison	35%	65%
Colin Altevogt	30%	70%
Mark Ellington	30%	70%
Rick Weinheimer	25%	75%

Chapter 4: Crafting a Winning Culture

"We did hundreds of 'little things' in our program that eventually would add up to one Big Thing....an IHSAA State Championship."
- Chuck Koeppen

"Working with people is about relationships; working with younger people magnifies this."
- Colin Altevogt

We talked in chapter 3 about the slow buildup of little things that precipitates a sustained crescendo of success. For most coaches, the tipping point seemed to be when the athletes finally bought into the coach's training plan and message of hard work. In this chapter, we explore that phenomenon more deeply. Exactly what are those little things that build up to become a team culture? There's no conclusive answer, and it often requires a well-timed alignment of talent with a willingness to work hard. But there are some practical details we can learn from these coaches, ideas about the building blocks of team culture.

A running shoe is not much more than rubber, plastic, mesh, foam, and string. Put those together haphazardly and you have a pile of nothing. Put it together with care and design, and you can go for hundreds of miles. To end up with a whole that transcends the sum of its parts, let's take a closer look at the parts, and how to properly piece them together: with personal attention, with ritual, and with transparency.

The Power of Personal Attention

When we asked our coaches how they cultivated buy-in, they talked about workouts and race-day procedures, they talked about fun summer activities, but more than anything else they talked about authenticity and care. In Scott Lidskin's words, "I think kids 'buy in' when they know that you genuinely care about them as people and when they understand that we all have the same goals." Sam Rasmussen said, "There is no substitute for listening...I was always there for them." Zach Raber noted that there isn't any one magic bullet, but that "they need to know that you are all in. They need to know that if you're asking them to outwork the competition, then you'll do that as a coach as well." One way Raber establishes this trust is through personal attention during training. He often alters his training plan, tailoring a workout for a specific athlete's needs. "When it works, you've got that kid forever." Erhard Bell emphasized the effect of personal encouragement on an athlete's mental preparation for running. "Positive reinforcement is far superior to negative comments," he added.

High school coaches are not paid in the off seasons of summer and winter, but they view that time as a critical opportunity for both training and forging relationships, planning fun activities that will bring out their runners' personalities. To build a team culture that fuses hard work with fun, Chuck Koeppen rewarded anyone who would come run with the "Winter Warriors" by creating a Ping-Pong Parlor. "I would talk trash so all the kids wanted to beat me and shut me up! They would come back, day after day...but they had to run first! I remember playing Chris Walden when he was a little freshman. I used to 'beat him like a drum!' But he kept coming back, and coming back.

He became a great runner, and now he can kill me in ping-pong!"

Personal attention plays an especially important role on large teams. Koeppen began this process early and often: "I very seldom missed a middle school meet that involved kids from our school system." Showing up and talking to middle schoolers at Carmel's feeder schools was a way to keep them from defecting to soccer or to another area high school, keeping Carmel's pool of talent deep. Colin Altevogt makes sure that every coach knows the name of every single athlete. That may sound basic, but for a school whose team rosters consistently top 100, it's not uncommon for names to be overlooked.

One way that Mike Prow ensured that his athletes received personal attention was to run with them. Prow explained, "In 1990, when I took the Valparaiso job, I was only 32 years old and running as fast or faster than my athletes, so I would get valuable feedback by running all the workouts with them. In 1995, Brett Polizotto became my assistant coach, and he was faster than all, so we got more feedback. In 2002, Aaron Crague became my assistant and he was young and *the fastest* and could get good feelings or vibes by mixing it up with the runners." Prow and his assistant coaches maximized their time by actively participating with the runners in practice.

As for deepening those relationships, coaches of larger teams have to get creative. Mark Ellington acknowledges the difficulty of managing so many relationships, so he sets up support systems in which athletes are consistently, outwardly caring for one another. Each athlete fills out an index card with her name, locker number, close friends on the team, and a few other interests or favorite things. Managers shuffle the cards, and each athlete gets a randomly-chosen "secret buddy," to whom she pays close attention and finds ways to show support in secret. Managers record the buddies on a master list, and each week athletes provide some sort of small treat or note of encouragement or congratulations for their friend. At the last meet of the season (Culver/MIC), they have a "big reveal." Ellington credits his team's "secret buddy" tradition with fostering deeper connections between athletes of differing abilities.

The Power of Ritual

Ritual gets a bad rap. It is often billed as empty or conformist. But successful coaches use ritual as a tool for achieving the opposite: a team culture that is meaningful, even transcendent. We often think of rituals in the context of religion, but ritual can be any performed action that takes on a ceremonial importance. The world of distance running, with its cyclical training plans and repeated weekly workouts culminating in a race many call "the big show," is rife with opportunity for establishing rituals.

No coach specifically used the word "ritual" in our interviews, but the activities they shared often had the hallmarks of ritual. Campfires, canoe trips, team dinners, pre-race chants, warm-up routines...with repetition, these activities become steeped in tradition and take on a sense of importance. Even places and objects can become sacred in this context. Barrie Peterson emphasized his team's many annual trips. He took his varsity runners on overnight trips 3-4 times each summer, to see a Chicago Cubs game, go to a water park, to trails in Dowagiac, Michigan, or to visit downtown Indianapolis, running together in each location. Every year, Tim Ray's team travels to the same course for a Hokum Karum race—a cross country relay in which partners race in tandem. "We have times from each kid that has ever run it, and the kids get pumped for it, and we really use it as a gauge of not only our fitness level, but where we think we can end up."

Embracing ritual bestows places, objects, and even workouts with significance, turning the profane into the sacred. Brad Peterson capitalized on that power by reserving certain locations for certain hard workouts. "Long runs out at Griffin Road (kids looked forward to these runs, and also the drive there and back was fun with each other)...Kirkwood mile repeats or two-mile repeats. Kids loved going there and running fast." Steve Kearney mentioned workouts that were done only at team camp, and kids looked forward to them and talked about them all year, like rites of passage: a 20-mile run (18 for girls), and a 90-minute run in which athletes took turns leading, exploring wherever they pleased, and staying off marked trails as much as possible.

What can ritual do for a team? Perhaps most obviously, it creates a shared culture and leads to what sociologist Émile Durkheim calls a "collective effervescence," that electric energy we feel at a political rally or when watching the superbowl in a room full of our team's fans (Durkheim, 1912/2001). Karen DeVries and her team used *downtown* as a code word for the state meet. "It all went back to making it *downtown*," Devries said of her team's hard work. An ordinary word, in the shared culture of the Valparaiso girls, became a word imbued with meaning and endowed the state meet with a kind of hallowed import. DeVries was careful not to talk about the state meet too much, but the team's collective effervescence showed that it was on everyone's mind. Of course, "collective effervescence" can potentially be destructive (hazing and loss of inhibitions come to mind), but if coaches guard against these things, rituals can turn banal

activities—dressing for a race, a 6AM run in the dark—
into sources of deep joy and meaning. Sam Rasmussen
mused, "I think the times student athletes spend
together eating apples and popsicles, having picnics,
going camping, cooking morning breakfast, and
running together played a bigger role than maybe even
I would admit."

Rituals assimilate new runners into the group
more fully. Once you have participated in rituals, you
know you are in the group. You're part of the team
because you learned the chant, wore the uniform,
jumped in the lake at team camp. It's important for
coaches to play a hands-on role in establishing these
kinds of traditions to ensure they do not take a turn
toward exclusion, bullying, or hazing. With a coach's
guidance, ritual provides boundaries, giving runners a
procedure for handling the high pressure of race day,
and all its emotions. In the often tumultuous teenage
years, a team's consistent, daily practice rituals can
serve as tools for emotional release and for processing
life's changes.

Rituals help to crystallize a team's ideals. In the
shared world created by a team's rituals, goals and
ideals take on an amplified realness. When Ellington's
runners stretch their arms forward into a tunnel for
their teammates to run through, they inhabit a world
in which the team *really might* matter more to each
one than the individual self. When Raber's Carroll girls
adorn their faces with "war paint" before a race, they
inhabit a world in which they *could be* the fiercest team
in the state. Even if this alternate reality is an illusion,
every time they act on it, they pull what is real closer
and closer to their ideal. Many of our coaches
mentioned that their teams always run warm-ups and
cool-downs together. Disciplined adherence to this
ideal feeds a narrative: "We are a team that waits for
everyone before we begin." And after the race, "We

process our win or our loss together." Even if individual runners fall short, the narrative persists and continues to boost the team's reality toward its shared image of itself.

The Power of Transparency

The third common element of the coaches' experiences with cultivating a shared culture had to do with the way they talked openly to their runners. They tried to give a reason for everything they did. They shared with their runners all the data they could about the progress they had been making. They were explicit about the culture they wanted their teams to embody. In short, they were transparent.

Before Valparaiso girls' first state win, Karen DeVries struggled to convince her team to believe in her training plan. But she stuck to it, and she doubled down by explaining absolutely everything: "why we trained where we did, or why we ran 10 miles, mile repeats, fast morning runs, or 1200s on a very tough course." It wasn't until their 13th-place finish at the state meet in 1998 (In DeVries' estimation, far below that group's potential) that the team finally came to DeVries and said they were ready to train. "Once that decision was made, the whole atmosphere of the team changed. The team was working as a whole, everyone going in the same direction with the same goal." The following year they were state champions. DeVries credits God with blessing her and her team as they came together for that first big win. Here is how she describes that transcendent moment: "The one thing that stands out to me was at a point in the race shortly before the mile mark, I saw all 7 runners looking fresh and focused. At that point I knew God had it, and at that point I felt the most humbled because something bigger than me was unfolding. God carried the team

41

that day, as all the other times, whether we won or not."
DeVries' runners had been willing to work hard daily to
prepare for that day in part because she had
relentlessly explained the purpose behind their
training. And, in her words, "God blessed our efforts."

Rick Weinheimer also relied on transparency to
build a shared team goal. Even the team's fun trips and
camps were oriented around educating the runners on
the physiological effects of various workouts. He
pinpointed that education as the biggest motivating
factor for his runners. "They know what benefits they
are getting from the workout each day, and that
encourages them to do their best and get the most out
of each workout." Colin Altevogt, who first coached as
an assistant under Weinheimer, agrees with his former
mentor that team culture depends on a training
program that makes sense to the athletes: "I spend a lot
more time crafting our training plan for the team than
I do coming up with any big motivational techniques or
doctrines. I think that a good training plan is
motivating enough if it is constructed well to display
the improvement of the athletes on a regular basis."

When that training works, transparency helps it
to snowball. When athletes have made any sort of
progress at all, their coaches make every effort to point
it out to them using hard data. They keep records of
workout results over the years, and they pull them out
at practice to let athletes see their progress. Altevogt
explains, "In cross country, we track all of their times
and distances (plus pace per mile), and we print out the
results each time. We also list their distance and pace
per mile from the same week the year prior. Each
athlete, regardless of ability level, has a side-by-side
tracking of what they did if they were on the team the
previous season." Joe Brooks sifted through workout
and meet data looking for ways to "spin" it so that
runners could see progress. "Any big wins or

outstanding meets can go a long way to make athletes believe they can run faster and be a part of a winning team," he says. He's not talking about deception, but simply being relentlessly focused on the positive.

Staying positive seems to get easier with copious, meticulous record-keeping; the more you keep track of, the more you can find small improvements. Data tracking is a lot of work. But according to our coaches, it is overwhelmingly worth it. Steve Lewark reminded us that data can give runners a sense of perspective about their role in the legacy of a program. In his detailed write-ups, he often pointed out to an athlete when they were running times that compared to top athletes of the past. "They could see that they were running workouts similar to the best we have had in the past and were running meets in a time very similar to what our past runners did. This would give them the confidence that they could compete with the best."

Great coaches are also transparent in the way of gospel preachers. They understand the weight of their words and often believe it's their calling to state explicitly the beliefs and values of their program. Raber advised, "You must be as relentless about talking about what you feel is success as you are about the workouts you put forth. You have to constantly 'fill the cup' of all of your athletes." Erhard Bell even codified his principles for success into what he calls "The Bell Doctrine," organizing his team's values into a written list. Chuck Koeppen preached—and is still preaching—team unity: "Everything that we did was centered around TEAM. I am not sure that we ever could have won anything without this philosophy. It is a necessary ingredient of all great teams, in any sport....you have to have it! In about every year that I was at Carmel HS, we had it in spades. We were Family!"

When runners have a sense that together they are a family, that they are building something that will endure even after they graduate, that they are personally cared for, then the mundane "little things" can become powerful bonds that elevate teams to great heights. In the words of sociologist Émile Durkheim (1912/2001), "Within a crowd moved by a common passion, we become susceptible to feelings and actions of which we are incapable on our own. And when the crowd is dissolved, when we find ourselves alone again and fall back to our usual level, we can then measure how far we were raised above ourselves" (p. 157).

Chapter 5: Autonomy

"This is their team. My goal is only to provide guidance."
- Erhard Bell

On a summer evening in a suburb northwest of Fort Wayne, sweaty elementary-aged kids in shorts and tee shirts gather on the grassy campus of Carroll High School. They guzzle water bottles and try not to fall over as they balance on one foot, attempting to copy the stance of the teenager who is demonstrating a standing quad stretch. One teenager answers a parent's question, while another retrieves a band-aid for a child who has fallen and scraped her knee. This is Carroll's cross country camp for kids, and during Zach Raber's tenure as coach it was run entirely by high schoolers. Raber was there to supervise, but he wasn't exactly running the show—his work had been done ahead of time, training his runners and equipping them to take the lead. He had appointed team captains, who were expected to plan the camp, delegate responsibilities to other team members, and communicate effectively with children, families, and each other so the event would run smoothly. "It was a total pressure situation for them," Raber recalls of the annual week-long event, which served as a major pipeline for bringing future runners to the Carroll team.

Raber had confidence that his experienced runners would rise to the occasion, and he gave them a chance to lead. What is striking about this philosophy is that it holds the athlete in such high esteem. No coach seems to fit squarely into just one philosophy, but we got an overwhelming sense that all of these legendary coaches viewed young people as fellow human beings to be respected, not lumps of clay to be molded or controlled. Many still appreciate an authoritative "old-school" leadership style—at least sometimes—but that style was infused with what we are calling a high view of young people, one that gives them a voice and generally assumes the best about them.

Psychologists call this approach "autonomy-supportive," meaning that it provides a structure in which young people are given power to act on their own ideas (Reeve, 2009). It minimizes attempts to control their behavior from above, and instead comes under them to support their growth into intrinsically motivated leaders. Indiana's top cross country coaches didn't all give their athletes as much freedom as Raber did, but they all held their athletes in high regard.

What is a High View of Young People?

Respect for Individuals

We noticed that our coaches seemed to regard their teenaged athletes as emerging adults with legitimate personal lives and differing priorities. They saw runners in their real-world contexts, holistically, as people with responsibilities to their families and their academics and to other pursuits. Tim Ray pointed out that in high school sports, you don't get to handpick athletes to come train intensely under perfect conditions. "Those runners have different levels of commitment, motivation, and determination. They come from different socioeconomic backgrounds. Kids that have a job after practice because they have to pay for shoes and clothes are mixed with those that are driving brand new cars at age 16. All of those kids come out for different reasons, which range from running so they don't have to have a job, to trying to earn a scholarship."

These coaches perform a great balancing act, giving voice to the athletes' personal goals and priorities while pushing them to grow in their commitment to the team and to see what's possible, beyond what they had hoped. Steve Kearney makes it a point to recognize his athletes for their accomplishments outside of running, even if those other endeavors sometimes take time away from his sport. "Sometimes that can seem counterproductive, like when they miss a meet to perform with a musical group," he said. "But it lets them know you are interested in them as a person."

Steve Lewark stayed intentional about how he communicated with his athletes. Lewark said, "Being older when I began coaching (48), and being an accountant, [a position] in which I had to work with many different types of people, I am calmer than many coaches. I never yell at my teams, just try to encourage them." Lewark had a steady and respectful presence with his athletes.

High Expectations

When adults see kids as people with inherent potential, their expectations become higher. By "higher," we don't mean that they become more demanding and hard to please. All great coaches expect hard work and excellent performance, but a high view of athletes goes further than winning or achieving benchmarks. Often coaches are measured on the external success of their athletes. But with a high view of their athletes, these coaches' hopes for their runners go deeper, guiding them toward growth and character development. They preach mental toughness, commitment to teammates, living consistent and ordered lives, and setting goals for nutrition and sleep. They preach community and self-sacrifice. They expect teammates to work hard out of love and respect for each other. Then they step back and let the kids live up to these high expectations.

A Lack of Micromanagement

With such high hopes for personal growth and character development, you might expect these coaches to be crafting goals and measuring personal growth the way they measure PRs. But overwhelmingly they don't. It turns out that having a high view of young people also means it doesn't make sense to try and control or micromanage them like you would train a pet. We asked our coaches if and how they measure an athlete's personal growth, and we kept getting answers like "No," "Nothing formal," "I may work on this in the future," and "I feel like the worst coach ever reading these questions, because I don't do much of this!" They don't keep tabs on any of these things. Instead, they just keep their eyes open. They stay mindful of the big-picture goals for their runners' lives. Joe Brooks informally measured personal growth by "observing changes in attitude, work ethic, running performance over a period of time. I've had runners who had never made the honor roll improve to always making the honor roll. I've had freshmen whose PR for 5K is 21:00, and when they are a senior their PR is 16:00. I've had runners who have had a difficult home life, and they have gone to college and become successful in life." External measures can still provide evidence of the hoped-for internal growth.

What Does Autonomy Look Like?

That lack of micromanagement works itself out in the way coaches give their athletes ownership of their team. The kids' camp wasn't the only way Raber gave autonomy to his athletes. He also put the captains in charge of organizing Friday night team dinners, initiating team warm-ups and cool-downs at meets, and organizing teammates for Sunday long runs on their own during the season. "I was there to supervise and fix any mistakes, but these things were all up to the captains," he said. Raber and his assistant coach Mike Barnes even gave athletes a voice when it came to the training. "We oftentimes would come to practice with several potential workouts. Based on the feeling of the groups, we would change our plans. If an athlete thinks they have input, then they will respond better." You might think this approach would lead to chaos or lowered standards, but as Raber explained, "This sport is all about confidence. If our athletes are confident in what they are doing in practice, then they will be confident in their races." Far from a *laissez-faire* "anything goes" environment, Carroll's student-led program has developed a consistent ethos of high expectations. Raber gave his athletes autonomy.

In his book *Drive*, Daniel Pink distinguishes between autonomy and independence. Pink explained, "Autonomy...is different from independence. It's not the rugged, go-it-alone, rely-on-nobody individualism of the American cowboy. It means acting with choice— which means we can be both autonomous and happily interdependent with others" (Pink, 2011, p. 88). Giving kids, especially older athletes, responsibility for team operations develops interdependence alongside individual confidence.

The Role of Captains

We asked how coaches select team captains, and their answers were split, with half of them choosing not to name captains at all. Those who did chose very carefully, making sure that captains had the experience and the right mindset to lead their peers. Those who

49

did not name captains gave compelling reasons for their decision.

Mike Prow never had captains. "I didn't want any runner to have that extra pressure or have to live up to expectations." Prow always elevated the team over the individual, so to prop up a couple of specific individuals as being more important leaders than others was inconsistent with his team-first philosophy. Eric Kellison shared a similar sentiment: "I never labeled anyone as a captain ever, period! Some guys were better leaders than others. I felt like it was my job as a coach to lead the team."

Early in Rick Weinheimer's career, he would name team captains a year ahead of time, either by vote or by coach's choice. But he found that it "seriously limits our leadership, because kids feel they are not expected or welcomed to be leaders if someone else has the title. Often someone I expect to be a good leader is not so good, and often someone I least expect becomes an important leader and model." So he did away with labeling captains. Similarly, Scott Lidskin does not have captains either. "We believe that all of our athletes should be leaders." To Weinheimer and Lidskin, naming captains sends the message that leadership is reserved for a few select individuals and not expected or welcomed of the others.

Mark Ellington's philosophy on team captains changed over time. He told us, "We do not name captains. In the first couple of seasons, I felt pressured to name captains because that had been done previously. I truly didn't find value in naming individuals as captains when so many athletes could make contributions and there seemed to be too much drama associated with who would be named. After two seasons, I stopped naming captains. My position was, 'If you want to be a captain, behave and act that way, and you'll be perceived as a captain by your peers. You don't need me to confer the title upon you.'"

Tim Ray does name captains, but he treats the selection process as something fluid throughout the season. Ray said, "Captains are usually selected at the start of the year, but can change depending on how their leadership is valued. I have had some captains not finish out the year as captains, and others that were not initially named captain be named captain in the middle of the season." Ray allows for the possibility that leaders will emerge over the course of the season.

Chuck Koeppen named captains, but he really emphasized the leadership responsibility of the entire senior class. He explained, "We always kind of felt like we 'go the way the seniors go.' Great senior leaders....we were money. If not, well, not so much."

Despite their very different views on the role of team captains, all of our coaches tried to create an environment where everyone on the team could contribute to a collective leadership. Their desire to keep leadership opportunities open is further evidence of the high view they take of their athletes' potential.

Accepting Feedback

Most of our coaches are quick to listen to athletes' feedback, stepping into the role of attentive guide whenever possible. Even on the specifics of training, and even in the middle of a workout, good coaches want feedback. Steve Kearney, who tries to leave as much as possible up to the athletes, pointed out that "experienced athletes know themselves better than we can by observation." Tim Ray listens with discernment, keeping in mind an athlete's maturity and re-evaluating the training based on their complaints. "This doesn't mean that...we do whatever they want to do or change things automatically; it's just reevaluated," said Ray. "Communication is one of the major components of training that we stress to our kids every year. High school kids may be immature at times, but when they become involved in the sport, they do know their bodies."

This form of autonomy doesn't seem to diminish the coaches' leadership or damage their authority. Our coaches did not seem to feel that opening themselves up to athlete feedback put them at the mercy of the athletes' whims or weakened their training plans. On the contrary, it seemed to foster receptivity on the part of the athletes and allow coaches to have a greater influence on young runners. Josh Fletcher said, "If they feel their voice matters, they are more likely to 100% commit. I welcome athletes who want to know *why* we are doing certain workouts. Part of my job is to educate my runners in case they are a coach or leader someday. My athletes don't always agree with my program but they clearly know that it's well thought out and meticulously implemented and that I'm passionate about it." Rick Weinheimer adapts individual runners' training days "constantly," but most of them seem to understand the big picture and are willing to go along with the coach's plan. In other words, being willing to listen, and doing so often, leaves him with a program that many athletes are ready to buy into. And once athletes have bought in, they lead others to do so as well, reinforcing the whole team's commitment to the training plan.

Weinheimer gives a lot of responsibility to his athletes, and so he spends a great deal of time preparing them for such responsibility. All of these coaches talked about or implied the importance of teaching runners about scientific training, but Weinheimer seemed to emphasize explicit educational time more than any other coach. He spoke about educating his runners so they will understand the "hows and whys" of everything they do and can then take ownership and lead others. "We start each year's educational process at team camp by holding two (sometimes three) educational (note taking) sessions each day. In addition, our top tier of runners will often ask to stay up after lights out and have an extra session that is beyond the perspective of the team in general. This is often advanced leadership and advanced training. During the season we continue our educational sessions twice a week, building on previous knowledge and introducing more information related to racing and competition." Weinheimer offers a week-long camping trip to all juniors and seniors for the purpose of developing their leadership skills. "Generally, [team leaders] seem to respect the fact that I give them ownership but also understand that I am a resource person that can give them feedback and advice." In this way, giving voice to individual athletes strengthens the collective voice of the team, creating mutual commitment and shared goals.

In what at first may seem like a totally opposite approach from the Raber-style autonomy, Joe Brooks told us he has never asked an athlete for feedback on a workout, and Scott Lidskin said he listens but he rarely makes changes to workouts. Yet in digging deeper, we found that these coaches do give athletes a voice, although they rely a bit more on observation to inform their decision-making. Lidskin described the more personal aspects of training, like developing mental toughness, as a "constant conversation" with his athletes, and he emphasized the importance of "understanding the uniqueness of each athlete." Brooks told us that he made workout adjustments at least weekly, depending on what runners seemed to need: "There are always certain runners who enjoy certain types of workouts better. So in a sense I knew what our runners needed and liked...Sometimes we felt our runners needed more rest, more distance, more speed, better finishes, etc. So we adjusted our workouts each week if needed."

Whether the coaches adhered to a traditional, authoritative model or a more casual and democratic one was not important; what mattered was how the coaches viewed the athletes. A high view of young people was a common denominator with all our coaches. In their words about giving their athletes autonomy and respect, we saw a zoomed-out approach to developing young people. Giving leadership responsibility and valuing athletes' individual feedback helps create a self-sustaining program that belongs to all those who invest in it, not just to the head coach. Rather than possessive micromanagement, we saw a sort of "this-is-bigger-than-me" philosophy. Demonstrating to athletes that their team's success is up to them—by making so much of what happens truly up to them—empowers them to work hard, work together, and take initiative. As Daniel Pink (2011) puts it, "We're born to be players, not pawns. We're meant to be autonomous individuals, not individual automatons" (p. 106).

Chapter 6: Mentors and Personal Connections

"The DAC coaches get together and talk often, and I am always picking their brains for ideas and training tips." - Tim Ray

Have you ever had the feeling that championship coaches are members of some exclusive club where they share their secrets of success? If so, you'd be half right: every single coach featured in this book has personal connections to at least some (if not most) of the other 18 coaches. It is a well-established club, yet it's anything but exclusive. In an age of easy access to scientific information about distance training, you might think our statistical criteria for inclusion in this book would turn out a more widespread and diverse group. So why did we end up with groups of friends, people who had coached together, and even a father-son pair? Many of our coaches are from larger schools in well-resourced communities, advantages which put them in a more exclusive position in the eyes of some. But there's more to it than where they coach. A significant reason for the personal connection phenomenon is the coaches' tendency to cultivate mentorships, not only with their own athletes, but also with others in their field.

In chapter 3 we mentioned the 10,000 hour rule made famous in Malcolm Gladwell's book *Outliers*. Many readers misunderstood Gladwell's purpose in using that number, thinking it meant you'll achieve greatness if only you can put in 10,000 hours of hard work. Yet in an interview with Stephen Dubner on Freakonomics radio, Gladwell further explained, "To me, the point of 10,000 hours is, if it takes that long to be good you can't do it by yourself ... If there is an incredibly prolonged period that is necessary for the incubation of genius, high performance, elite status of one sort or another, then that means there always has to be a group of people behind the elite performer making that kind of practice possible" (Dubner, 2016). Our coaches had many such supportive relationships.

Strong Ties

Barrie and Brad Peterson, as father and son, have what sociologists call a "strong interpersonal tie" (Granovetter, 1973). They are in each other's inner circles, and the tie between them is strengthened and reinforced by the fact that so many of Barrie's acquaintances also know Brad, and vice versa. In addition to Barrie being Brad's father and his high school cross country coach, they also coached together. They partnered up for two years at Northrop HS, before Brad went on to coach at Concordia Lutheran HS and later at Indiana Tech, where the tables turned and Barrie became Brad's assistant coach. Brad's relationship with his dad has had immeasurable impact on his own success. Brad is also good friends with Josh Fletcher and Eric Kellison, two other coaches from our list, and with Derek Leininger, co-author of this book. Brad Peterson was the best man in Fletcher's wedding, and he credits both Fletcher and Kellison with mentoring him in coaching and other walks of life.

Karen DeVries had the good fortune of consistent support as she transitioned from her own running career into coaching others. She caught a love of running and of hard work from John Martin, her high school coach. Then, as a coach, she worked under an athletic director who had also been a state championship cross country coach at Valparaiso HS, Sam Rasmussen (also featured in this book). He was not only her boss but also her mentor. "I could go into his office anytime, and he was always very welcoming and ready to listen to my ideas or concerns and offer advice...He understood the hours it took, and I could talk to him about running so easily because he had already accomplished what I had set out to do." She could feel Rasmussen's commitment to student-athletes and his genuine happiness in her success. "The first time we won state, Sam was right there at the finish line with the biggest smile that I will never forget!" Were it not for his support, DeVries believes she may have given up altogether and missed out on "the many blessings, opportunities, and personal growth experiences God had in store for me." Rasmussen agrees, describing their relationship as "very good friends who tried to collaborate to make [the] program the best it could be."

Steve Kearney, Steve Lewark, and Chuck Koeppen were college roommates and teammates at Ball State. Kearney also became good friends with the famous runner and author Hal Higdon. They never worked together formally, but their friendship taught Kearney much that helped him to become a better coach. Joe Brooks lists Mike Prow among his good friends and someone who encouraged him to get into coaching. Steve Lewark credits Lane Custer, the head track and field coach at West Lafayette High School, for bringing him into coaching and helping him along. Colin Altevogt's father, Brad, and sister, Lynn, are also experienced runners and coaches, and Colin is a close friend of Derek Leininger; frequent conversations with his family and with Leininger often revolve around coaching and training. Strong ties provide support and shape who we become. Many of our coaches benefited from strong ties with their own former coaches, mentors, and close friends.

Weak Ties

We can't all have partnerships with our fathers and friendships with our bosses, but you don't have to have strong ties to an intimate circle of coaches in order to achieve success. Altevogt's daily interactions and strong ties with coaches have certainly helped him, but perhaps even more influential to his development of coaching expertise were relationships classified as "weak ties." Weak ties are acquaintances with people who move primarily in different social circles and can thus introduce each other to new information and opportunities. Altevogt gleaned wisdom as he worked as an assistant to both Rick Weinheimer at Columbus North HS and Erhard Bell at Carmel HS before becoming the head boys' coach at Carmel in 2014. Their social circles and life experiences are mostly separate, so there was plenty for Altevogt to learn from them. This idea held true across our research. When we asked our coaches to name people who influenced their careers, most of them pointed to weak ties. In 2014, Chesterton coach Tim Ray knew his 4x800-meter relay team could be great, so he built up a network of weak ties with coaches he didn't know personally but who had mid-distance expertise, reaching out to Derek Leininger (Snider HS) and to Zach Raber (Carroll HS), who had defeated Chesterton the year before. Ray's team became state champions that spring thanks in part to advice from people who, at the time, he barely knew!

Some coaches seem to be particularly adept at forging both strong and weak ties between coaches, a role sociologists would call a "social entrepreneur" (Praszkier & Nowak, 2011). The most obvious social entrepreneur of the group is Chuck Koeppen, who is (not coincidentally) the winningest high school cross country coach in Indiana history. Koeppen coached and mentored Mark Ellington, Carmel's current head girls' cross country coach. He mentored Erhard Bell as his assistant for four years, before Bell succeeded him as the boys' head coach. He mentored Joe Brooks, who, as a college senior, ran with Koeppen's team while student-teaching at Clay Middle School. He mentored a young Rick Weinheimer, who did a one-month coaching internship with Koeppen and then attended every coaching clinic session Koeppen presented over the next three decades. Ellington, Bell, Brooks, and Weinheimer all went on to win multiple team state titles in cross country.

Koeppen, for his part, learned plenty from those coaches he "mentored," and from many others he's met. He named as his biggest influences his former coach, Ken Pifer at Valparaiso HS; Wilber Veatch, for whom he student-taught; and Joe Newton, arguably the most successful high school cross country coach in US history. Newton recently retired at the age of 87, after six decades of coaching at York High School in Illinois. Koeppen studied Newton's books and credits *The Long Green Line* in particular with giving him great ideas that led to the success of Carmel's program. Wisdom shared from across the Illinois-Indiana state line helped Koeppen build a powerhouse program and in turn spread information and ideas to all the coaches Koeppen has influenced—those profiled in this book, and hundreds of others who have attended his talks at coaching clinics.

An Unseen Network of Support

Less obvious connections influenced our coaches' development too. Many coaches began running thanks to encouraging physical education teachers. Mark Ellington's sixth-grade P.E. teacher, who also happened to be the middle school cross

59

country coach, was none other than Bobby Cox, the current commissioner of the Indiana High School Athletic Association. In Indiana it should come as no surprise that several of our coaches first got into running to be in shape for other sports, especially basketball. Rick Weinheimer wanted to make the basketball team, and since the basketball coach also coached cross country, he tried it out. Scott Lidskin ran only because the basketball coach threatened to cut him from the roster if he didn't! Joe Brooks began cross country to prepare for basketball at Rushville High School (Good thing he did—He made the basketball team and ended up playing in the semi-state game at Butler University's Hinkle Field House). Tim Ray ran because his parents wouldn't let him play football. Many of our coaches learned from basketball and football coaches how to treat athletes, and then they studied hard to put those lessons into the context of distance running. Indiana's successful cross country tradition turns out to be built on the older tradition of our state's high regard for high school athletics in general.

As coaches, less visible support structures were no less crucial than relationships to the experts. Coaches depended on enthusiastic assistants, supportive spouses, and family members who were willing to sacrifice their own Saturdays for the team. Rasmussen credits much of his success to assistant coach Mike Polite, whose own running ability challenged the athletes and brought their training to a new level. Mike Prow relied on assistants Brett Polizotto and Aaron Crague. Joe Brooks praised assistant coach Dennis McNulty, who is a beloved and legendary coach in his own right. We wish there were some way to give credit to all the people who influenced these 19 coaches and thus affected the trajectory of distance running in Indiana, but there are simply too many to name. The lesson is clear: to become great at something you need to build relationships and learn from others. Mine your existing network for support, and then reach out to experts, who are often surprisingly willing to help out. The most successful coaches are those who are securely situated in a dense web of supportive relationships.

Chapter 7: Abundance Mindset and Competition

"It takes at least five guys to make a TEAM."
- Mike Prow

William Muir, an evolutionary biologist at Purdue University, studied the productivity of egg-laying chickens in the 1990s. He observed hens over six generations, counting the eggs they produced. He left aside a flock of nine average chickens, and in a parallel flock he undertook to breed super-productive chickens. Each generation, in this experimental flock, he selected the most productive individual chickens for breeding. You might reasonably expect that at the end of the experiment the selectively bred flock would be much more productive than the average flock. Yet after six generations, the average chickens were healthy and had become much more productive. In the super flock, however, six of the nine chickens were dead. They had pecked each other to death, and the productivity of the three bedraggled survivors had plummeted (Muir and Wilson, 2016).

Thankfully, nobody is talking anymore about literal selective breeding for humans, but often successful and talented people approach social interactions and athletic pursuits in a similar way, like superchickens pecking the competition to death instead of maximizing the potential of the whole flock. In just about every aspect of our society, from games on the playground to how businesses operate, it exists: the idea that if there is a winner there has to be a loser. To put it in the modern vernacular, "Not everyone gets a trophy." And that can be true in competitive running, which produces a largely objective hierarchy of numbers and rankings. These coaches remain very competitive, yet in important ways they have avoided this superchicken mentality.

When we talked about our coaches' social ties in the previous chapter, you may have noticed a remarkable amount of information sharing. Not only do these coaches share their training plans and philosophies in presentations and professional coaching clinics, but they also call each other for advice and share their own practices with others, even if their ideas are not fully developed or proven. When Tim Ray emailed Zach Raber for help with his 4x800 strategy, he was asking a competitor for tips! When I (Derek) was a new coach, I called several of the coaches featured in this book and asked to meet with them and pick their brains. I sat down and had conversations with Brad Peterson, Barrie Peterson, Chuck Koeppen, Eric Kellison, Mike Prow, Colin Altevogt, Josh Fletcher, Rick Weinheimer, Scott Lidskin and Zach Raber. Most of them did not know me very well at that time, but they all willingly shared their expertise. They demonstrated that same openness when they agreed to participate in this book project. Nobody is guarding their secrets. None of these coaches believed that their success depended on the failure of everyone else.

The Abundance Mindset

One partial reason for this openness may be an acknowledgement that, as John L. Parker, Jr., puts it in *Once a Runner* (1978/2010), there is no secret to distance running success beyond "that most unprofound and sometimes heart-rending process of removing, molecule by molecule, the very tough rubber that comprised the bottoms of his training shoes" (p. 229). Still, successful coaching requires plenty of knowledge and skill, and we think the reason they are willing to share it is that they possess what Stephen

Covey calls an "abundance mindset" (Covey, 1989). They understand that success isn't a zero-sum game: there's always some to go around, and if we build on the small innovations of others, we make each other better. With an abundance mindset, coaches are more willing to cooperate with each other, share training details, and define success on their own terms.

Think about how rare this mindset is in a sports world where competition is the point, where teams must hide their playbooks to protect their chances of winning. Distance running by nature may allow for this kind of openness more than, say, football. But it still includes a lot of strategy and planning that can mean the difference between reaching your potential and bottoming out. So it is remarkable that the Indiana running community is one in which Joe Brooks can lightheartedly quote his fellow Warren Central coach: "As Dennis McNulty always said, 'Coaching is about thievery.' We stole many ideas over the years and our runners bought into them." When Barrie Peterson added his son Brad to the coaching staff at Northrop, he didn't micromanage him out of a need for control. Instead, he gave him autonomy and was willing to learn from him, and it paid off in a big way. This openness to building relationships and mentoring others has been an essential factor in the development of all our coaches. That won't happen for chickens, but for successful human coaches, embracing an abundance mindset seems to be a hallmark of legendary distance running programs.

Competition and Cooperation

A mindset of abundance doesn't necessarily make "competition" a dirty word. As you'll see in Chapter 9, winning still helps to define success for many of these coaches. In fact, competition and cooperation don't have to be opposing values. In their book *Top Dog*, Po Bronson and Ashley Merryman explain how in ancient Greece, competitive sport actually fostered the development of democracy. The concept of *aretas* was "the virtue of excellence found through competition." Competitors were supposed to develop this virtue through hard work, prove they had it, and then use it "for the good of all." Fair competition and sportsmanship give dignity to participants regardless of their social status at birth. Competition led to more equality, not less (Bronson & Merryman, 2013). And so competition and cooperation work together in our sport.

It is therefore unsurprising that the coaches' approach to teaching competitiveness to their athletes is quite nuanced. They encourage and enjoy competition against other teams, but always underscored by respect and sportsmanship. Our sport is conducive to competition between teams and individuals because we can find so many things to measure: times, places, team scores, PRs, etc. In many ways, a competitive spirit is a desirable trait. Some of the coaches even listed their own "competitiveness" as a trait that has made them successful. But with such measurable results, competition between teammates is bound to arise, and to this our coaches take varied approaches. Most appreciate the benefits of a healthy rivalry, as long as it is clear that both runners are competing for the good of the team rather than thinking only of themselves. Zach Raber tries to channel his runners' competitive edge by encouraging competition within the context of a cooperative team: "I truly believe you can get kids excited about winning but it's *very* difficult to teach them a killer instinct. I'd rather have a competitor and teach them cooperation than a cooperator and teach them competitiveness."

Rick Weinheimer tends to let rivalries play out naturally: "I've had boys who have been very successful keeping track of who wins more often, and I've had runners who practically slowed down in races because they mentally believed in the team 'pecking order.' A healthy benefit to the team lies somewhere in between those two extremes." But for girls, he is more careful. "For some reason it's been harder for our girls to battle it out up front and to continue as part of a healthy team. Unfortunately, the girl that begins to get beaten by her teammate more often slowly slides backwards in her performances."

Others who have coached girls echoed this concern. Scott Lidskin, who has spent his entire career coaching girls, has seen competition sometimes become a hindrance to his team's cooperation, so he discourages it: "We prefer that teammates work together to race as fast and place as high in meets as they can, as opposed to fighting against each other to see who is faster," he said. Mark Ellington finds that encouraging pairs or small groups of runners to "get better together" helps to diminish resentment and stave off feelings of favoritism. He often encourages individuals or small groups of similarly-abled runners to step up and be competitive, both in races and in workouts. He displayed the abundance mindset perfectly when he told us, "Encouraging an individual runner to be competitive and to continue to be aggressive does not have to come at the expense of another runner's progress."

The abundance mindset can help coaches of both genders, too. Steve Lewark started out as the boys' cross country coach at West Lafayette, and after four years he began coaching the girls as well. When he combined the two programs, he was careful not to make the transition about comparing or competing, instead treating them as part of one program. His approach led to greater success for both teams. Lewark explained, "This increased our numbers, as boys wanted to come out because of girls and girls wanted to come out because of boys. The more numbers we had, the better we did." The girls, who had never been to the state meet, improved rapidly under Lewark's direction. By the third year, they placed fifth in state, and continued making state-meet appearances almost every year, with six more podium finishes. When the boys saw their success, they bought into Lewark's training program too, since he had encouraged a mindset of abundant success within the program. The boys have since made it to state eight of the last thirteen years, with two podium finishes.

Tim Ray has never glossed over the competitive nature of his team's tournament roster, but he has stressed the idea that runners are better together. "What I want for each kid that comes through our program is to feel as though they were a part of something bigger. Family is what is stressed in our program. They will always be a member of the Chesterton High School distance family." Ray's comments sum up the overall mindset of Indiana's legendary coaches. We are competitors for certain, but we are all part of something bigger, a tradition in which we make each other better and success is abundant.

Chapter 8: That Winning Feeling

"I was sky high ... I was in love with coaching. I think I did a victory lap by myself outside the stadium and cried."
- Brad Peterson

The first time Scott Lidskin's Westfield girls won a state title, in 1998, he wasn't sure how to react. He and his team had planned and planned for a chance to win, but when it finally happened it was surreal. "We didn't really know what to do or how to act....we didn't plan for how to respond to winning, so we were just able to enjoy the moment."

That unguarded moment of celebration and reward was a common experience for our coaches. It was refreshing to hear this group of experts waxing nostalgic about their earliest wins, still seemingly blown away by the feeling. Eric Kellison described it as "incredible...a storybook season." Chuck Koeppen said, "It was one of the greatest days of my life!" What's more, they mostly talked the same way about their later successes too. Kellison said of his four top-5 podium team finishes, "Each time was fun, and the satisfaction was nearly the same." Steve Kearney's runners set three state records in the 4x800-meter relay, and "each seemed as thrilling as the others."

Under Pressure

While our coaches unanimously agreed that winning felt as wonderful as they had hoped it would, it's true that sometimes that feeling was more like relief than joy. Joe Brooks described Warren Central's first team win in 2005 as "jubilance," but the following year, with 5 of his top 7 runners returning, their win felt different. "It was as if a boulder had been lifted off our shoulders," he remembered. High expectations can generate a pressure to win that changes the experience. We often hear championship coaches share that building success is easier than sustaining it.

No one knows the pressure to keep winning like the coaches at Carmel, an affluent school with 5,000 students in grades 9-12, where the girls' swim and dive team has won an unbelievable 30 consecutive state titles, and the cross country teams have a realistic chance to win the state title every single year. Chuck Koeppen, who began building up Carmel's cross country program in the 1970s, recalls winning six titles in seven years early on. "We had sort of created a monster. People in and around the program were now only satisfied with first place." Some may be quick to criticize a community that puts such pressure on its young people, but Koeppen points out that sometimes expecting to win is simply an acknowledgement of the team's advantages. He felt relief when his über-talented 1987 girls' team won state, scoring a mere 19 points. "Sometimes you have a team that *should* win, and as a coach, you realize that and you just don't want to mess things up."

Recently retired Carmel girls' cross country coach Mark Ellington acknowledged feeling that pressure too. Ellington explained, "A small number of spectators want to see you win and continue a 'streak' or 'dynasty.' A much larger group would rather see you 'dethroned.'" Ellington took it in stride and managed expectations by focusing on improvement throughout the process rather than winning. Erhard Bell, who coached for nine years at Carmel (four years as an assistant coach and five years as a head coach), did not acknowledge the same pressure, however, choosing instead to keep his focus simply on personal bests and internal motivation in order to insulate his athletes from any external pressure to win.

Growing in Confidence

Not every coach felt added pressure from winning state, but winning had other effects. Steve Lewark, who kept on an even keel after winning, noticed that winning changed his team's culture. Now, it seemed to the runners, "anything was possible." Lidskin agreed: after winning, "every athlete became a bit more serious...had a bit more pep in her step." In other words, they grew confident. Zach Raber pointed out that this confidence is especially helpful if the winning group includes several younger runners, because winning allows the whole team to begin expecting bigger things. For this same reason, Chuck Koeppen credits his boys' first win in 1976 with paving the way for many future championships: "Our kids now believed it could be done, and they believed in the formula to our success."

In his first year at Valparaiso, Mike Prow's team finished fifth at the state meet. After that, Prow admitted, "Our goal was always to *win*." His teams developed the confidence that they could always compete with the best in Indiana, and over the next 10 years they won two state titles and finished in the top 5 eight times.

It isn't just the runners who reap confidence from a win. Brad Peterson was euphoric after his first 4x800-meter relay win because he felt validated. He had been coaching alongside his father Barrie, and they sometimes had disagreements about what was best for the team; but winning gave Brad confidence that he could coach. "I think I did a victory lap by myself outside the stadium and cried," he said.

Ellington credits his assistant coach Matt Wire with leveraging the Carmel girls' state championship wins to enlarge the team's goals, "giving all of us a bigger canvas to dream." Winning state gave athletes permission to hope for success on a national stage, and Wire encouraged talk about the possibilities. "Let's make noise at NXN" became a rallying cry, not a distant dream. As Josh Fletcher put it, winning "raised the success bar to a new level."

Recalibrating the Feeling

You might expect trophies to lose their luster for teams who are used to being the best or who feel extra pressure to win. But even after a combined 32 boys' and girls' cross country team state championships, winning for Carmel has retained its aura. "Every one of our state championships felt wonderful!" says Koeppen. Rick Weinheimer enjoyed the feeling of winning so much that after finishing third at Nike Cross Nationals in 2010—behind Arcadia (CA) and Fayetteville-Manlius (NY)—he found himself distracted and daydreaming about going back and getting pampered with Nike merchandise again the next year. To remind himself that his true goal was not to win but to develop each athlete according to his or her potential, Weinheimer met one-on-one with his slowest runner upon returning from the national meet, to talk about that runner's goals and training. "It was to help me keep from getting caught up in the 'winning is the only thing' mentality."

Developing the struggling runner is, it seems, the real source of that winning feeling. No matter how many wins a coach has experienced, it feels good to see kids making progress, reaching their goals. Colin Altevogt, who has played a role in championships both at Carmel and earlier at Columbus North as Rick Weinheimer's assistant coach, reasoned that "the ultimate joy comes from seeing the athletes achieve their success, so in that regard it has been great each time." Lidskin agreed that overcoming obstacles never gets old: "Every state title felt different based on the unique challenges that each team faced." Those unique challenges present themselves anew each year because of the developmental nature of high school sports.

The Amateur Ideal

Indiana loves its high school sports tournaments, in part because they allow communities to witness—and feel they are a part of—the magic of amateurism. When we watch professional sports, we are watching a well-oiled machine, carefully designed and highly funded for optimal performance. Youth sports have been somewhat professionalized, but in these coaches we saw that the amateur ideal is alive and well. The appeal of high school cross country is still largely the same as always: find a place to belong, work hard, and win or lose alongside lifelong friends.

Distance running lends itself well to this amateur ideal; even the professionals in our sport (with very rare exceptions) don't get rich from running. There is no real secret to success, so most high school coaches have as much access to training information as any expensive private coach. Running is low-cost, requiring little beyond a pair of shoes and a sidewalk. And it's accessible to almost anyone; even with the freedom to limit their rosters, most cross country coaches choose to keep anyone on the team who is willing to put in the work. Certainly inequities exist, such as having treadmills or indoor facilities for the winter, or living in a wealthy area where many families value youth sports and nutrition and have easy access to trainers and physical therapists. These are real advantages from which some of our coaches have benefitted. But as far as sports go, distance running is about as democratic as it gets.

Barrie Peterson praised the role that distance running plays in providing so many opportunities for meaningful growth and a sense of accomplishment, even without winning. Peterson spent his early coaching years at Fort Wayne Central High School, where the team's best cross country record during his tenure was 5 wins and 10 losses. "I called it my 'dime store' season—get it? 5 and 10, for those who recall Woolworth's Five and Dime!" After Peterson's many later wins with Northrop's track team, his feeling about those 5 small victories at Central HS rivals any championship memory. "I truly believe we were winners!" That winning feeling is, to some extent, tied up in the camaraderie that is particular to the amateur ideal of high school sports. "Many of those athletes remain friends to this day," remarked Peterson. Rick Weinheimer recalled attending the wedding of a runner who was part of a championship team. "Since that time he has gone to college, graduated from law school, and become a practicing attorney. Yet 15 years after the championship, 4 of his 6 groomsmen were high school teammates," Weinheimer noted. A championship isn't just a win; it's a win *together*. "True, achievements can never be taken away...but the friendships last forever."

High school runners, like athletes in every sport, have moved toward specialization in recent decades, and with it comes an implied need for year-round training, which does improve performance. But there persists an expectation among these coaches that high school teams are about something profoundly unprofessional—an operation made up of a community's kids. Hoosier coaches love that any community in the state could, potentially, send its runners to compete against the very best for a state title, a notion that has made it verboten to many in Indiana to suggest separating the cross country tournament into classes by school size, as most states now do. A one-class tournament limits the opportunities for multiple teams to win, but it also rarefies the experience, elevates the ideal, and gives the state a sense of cohesive community.

Collecting trophies feels good to these coaches because every win is an amateur win. It is kids using what they've been given, discovering their potential, making it work. As Sam Rasmussen told us, winning feels great "because we could turn to each other and say, 'I have done the best that I could do.'"

Enduring Wisdom

Chapter 9: Measuring Success

"We never talked about winning or losing. We talked about doing the best we could during practices, to prepare to be able to perform at our highest level."
- Sam Rasmussen

In Chapter 3 we discussed how success takes time and how long it took some of our coaches to reach the zenith of success in our sport. Of course, when we defined success for that chapter (and when we selected coaches for this book) we used a straightforward external definition of success: the state championship. But the coaches themselves had a more nuanced definition of success. Saying that "winning isn't everything" may sound cliché, but in exploring how great coaches measure success, we found advice that is intensely practical.

Focus on Process, Not Outcome

Sam Rasmussen and his athletes never talked specifically about winning or losing. Their focus was always on the process of preparation, not the outcome. Rasmussen explained, "Success can only be measured through oneself – did I make an effort to do my best?" While the outcome is subject to a number of uncontrollable variables, the process is something that a team can have complete control over. Several of our coaches acknowledged that the state meet is the single most obvious measuring stick for success, but they preferred to stay focused on what they could control: the process of getting there.

Colin Altevogt explained that when you value the process, the outcome often takes care of itself. "I try to be more process oriented rather than results based. A successful season occurs when the individuals on the team improve and learn to challenge themselves more than the previous season," he said. Scott Lidskin uses a four-question litmus test to measure the success of a season: "1. Did we stay healthy? 2. Did we reach our potential when it most mattered? 3. Did we enjoy the journey? 4. Did we improve as runners and people?" Three of Lidskin's questions are about the process, while only question 2 is about the outcome. Karen DeVries measured a season on her team's growth. "This growth comes in many different areas of the athlete's life, and in many different measurements. Each individual's growth is measured differently along with each season," she pointed out.

These coaches love to compete, and they love to win. But they have rejected a singular focus on results in favor of a big-picture approach. Focusing on the process does not mean ignoring objective results. It simply changes the way that you look at that data. Josh Fletcher measures success with one word: "Improvement! From one season to the next and from the beginning of the season to the end. I take pride in the fact that the majority of my athletes continue to improve throughout their high school career."

Focus on Internal Goals

Barrie Peterson defined success as "being the best that you can be at any given point in time, with the God-given talents and abilities with which you are blessed." His definition captures the subjective nature of success and the importance of not getting caught up in other people's expectations. In a sports world where standards are often based on media rankings, predictions, or message board chatter about the superstars, our coaches strive toward a different metric. Erhard Bell told us, "Coaches, I feel, should not be judged by the success of their top runners, but by those who are at the back of the pack," he said. Instead of worrying about the rankings, Bell focused solely on the athletes on his roster. His team's goal each year was that everyone achieve a 5K PR during each season. He also reviewed every athlete's personal goal card, meeting with runners individually (even when he had up to 130 runners!). "These items make everyone feel that they are part of the team, even if they are not on varsity."

Internal goals were important to Joe Brooks, too. He kept his team focused internally by emphasizing the motto "A Tradition of Success." He leveraged the success of previous Warren Central teams in order to create an internal expectation of excellence, without the distraction of outside expectations. His athletes made individual goals each year, but he always emphasized team goals and team improvements, grounding their individual goals in an understanding that they were carrying on a tradition as a team and leaving a legacy behind them.

Tim Ray has a specific workout he uses to teach his athletes about setting their goals internally. He waits until right after a race, as soon as the team returns to camp, and then he springs it on them: a stride workout, usually 6 or 7 x 200 meters. "I go a little old school on them," admitted Ray. "I say, 'We are going to run until I say stop.'" As they finish each stride, Ray "harps" on the importance of being mentally tough and giving your absolute all. He tells them they'll continue to sprint until everyone gives their all and is under 30 seconds. By the third repetition, kids begin to verbally encourage one another and say positive words to their struggling teammates. "It is amazing to watch," he said. They don't all break 30 seconds, and Ray is careful not to run them into the ground. but they all give everything they have. Later, when they return from a slow cool-down jog, Ray discusses the difference between internal and external motivation. He asks, "How is it possible for you to run what I asked when you had just given 'your all' in the race?" The runners are silent. Ray then explains that there was some external motivation from him, which had pushed them further. "Somehow, some way, their internal motivation needs to be greater than my external motivation if they want their absolute best. They have to believe that there is more, and they have to find it...I think it's very helpful to show young athletes that at some point they have done something that they did not think could be done. They can take that experience with them when those negative thoughts start to creep in, and be mentally tough to overcome."

Focus on the Athlete's Experience

"Remember the feeling!" Tim Ray told his team many times, reminding them of both the elation of success and the agony of defeat. Ray valued his own positive memories as an athlete, and he tried to coach his athletes toward a similar experience. He explained, "What drove me as an athlete was my desire to reach my dreams and the feeling I got when I did. That is what has driven me ever since. I want as many kids as possible to have that same feeling." What is notable about Ray's approach is that feelings are subjective. He isn't defining what their dreams should be. For Ray the quest for success always comes from the perspective of the athlete.

Similarly, Steve Kearney's hope was for each runner to reach success, whatever that meant to them. When we asked how he measures success, his response intrigued us. He said he looked at how many runners had come out for the team. Kearney explained, "The more athletes, the more backing the runners get from teammates, and the community becomes more aware of the program. I never took my job to be developing top-flight teams. I felt my job was to get as many kids to improve as I could. Some days the top kid could therefore be someone dropping from 24:00 to 23:00 [for a 5K] or someone that passes three or four opponents he had never beaten before. When a whole bunch of kids go into a week thinking about improving like this, they become supportive of each other." For Kearney, a larger group of enthusiastic runners would mean more positive experiences for those runners.

Focusing on the athlete's experience ahead of your own is not without its difficulties. Rick Weinheimer confided that each year he is "nagged by believing in all circumstances that I could have done more and we could have been a bit more successful." It's not simply that they could have achieved a more perfect score. It's that, when success means athlete-centered growth, there is always more to do, regardless of how many championships have been won. "Maybe that keeps me driven to work hard and to learn more and to improve every year," he said. Weinheimer has recently announced his retirement. "I know that I will look back at all those years with some satisfaction, but I will also wonder what could have been if I had done things a little better."

The Role of the State Meet

Given the emphasis on season-long improvement, internal goals, and an individualized definition of success, we wondered exactly what role the state meet plays in a coach's concept of how the season went. We asked two questions: one, "Is it possible to run terribly at the state meet and still feel like your season was a success?" And two, "Is it possible for a frustrating, discouraging season to be redeemed by one great state meet?" The first question got a unanimous "yes!" The response to the second was mixed.

Good Season, Bad State Meet

Several coaches remembered feeling that a season was successful despite a poor performance at state. Zach Raber's girls realistically expected to compete near the top in the 2008 championships, but they finished in 9th place. Yet Raber saw that day a level of effort and courage from his athletes that far exceeded the actual result. He explained, "If we focus on the effort instead of performance, then we have to be satisfied with where we finish." Erhard Bell agreed. "If one only bases success on a Championship, then we may very often be disappointed, which is not how it should be. The most important goal, I believe, is self-improvement, and if the majority of my runners achieve that goal, then we have success."

Sometimes it took a bit of time or perspective to consider the season a success. In 2009, Mark Ellington's first year as Carmel's girls' head coach, his team lost to Columbus North 96-178. "Columbus North ran a terrific race; nearly flawless. We would have been hard pressed to match them," he said. "Initially it was a complete failure. There's a feeling, if you're Carmel, and you don't bring home a state championship, that you are somehow a failure. I felt that way about our 2009 season for several years. I view it differently today. We were quite successful, but fell short of our final goal. There were some good lessons learned that day. How much wisdom do you gain if you never overcome adversity?" Rick Weinheimer agreed that of course a season can be successful without a great state meet. But he acknowledged that, emotionally, it can be hard to feel that way right after a loss. "I think generally that I judge too much off of the state meet," he admitted. When coaches say that winning isn't everything, they aren't claiming perfect zen enlightenment or sugarcoating life's harsh realities; they are stating what they know to be true, whether or not their feelings agree. It sometimes takes work to subordinate their feelings to what they know are their values.

Bad Season, Good State Meet

As for whether a good state meet can erase the negatives of a rough journey getting there, the question requires a little more thought. On the one hand, the state meet serves as confirmation that all of that improvement really was happening behind the scenes. Steve Lewark never knew what to expect of his 2014 girls' team. They ran inconsistently throughout the season, but they came together for a shocking 3rd place finish at state. In 2011, Karen DeVries' final year as a coach, her team struggled through the season, unsure if they would make it to state. "I cared about them and knew deep down what was most important for them and the experiences I wanted them to remember. That fueled me as a coach to continue to work hard for them, keep my head up, not only looking to God for guidance, but being positive for the team." They did make it to state, and ended up in 3rd place! "That kind of erased all the negatives of the season and brought the team together and helped them see that we are in this together and we all do care. It was special," DeVries recalls.

Joe Brooks' 2006 Warren Central team was crippled by pressure to live up to the previous year's success, making for a stressful season. Here's how Brooks tells it: "The pressure finally came to a head when we finished 4th at Culver and lost to Carmel by 60 points. The next Monday I met with only our top runners while Coach McNulty took everyone else.

Without talking much about Culver I made each runner do a long run, sending them out about every 3 minutes, and they had to run by themselves. When they got back, I talked to them about how did they like to run by themselves, and most said they didn't like it. I told them that is how the season has been going. Everyone is out for themselves, there is no 'I' in team. I gave each runner a clear bead for their Warrior necklace, so they could clear their conscience. We never lost again until the semi-state, to Franklin Central. We, however, ran lights-out at the 2006 state meet to win back-to-back state championships. Our season was saved." Lewark, DeVries, and Brooks had seasons marked with adversity but felt vindicated thanks to the state meet. Even so, they seemed, to some extent, to see the state meet as a valuable external indicator of a team's growth. Rather than seeing a great state meet as an uncharacteristic fluke that whitewashed the negatives of the season, these coaches felt great because they'd believed in their runners' potential all along.

Define Success for Yourself

About half of the coaches agreed that a great state meet could redeem a frustrating season, but what interested us most was that the majority answered in theoretical terms. Many said it has never actually happened to them because they don't think they've ever had a whole season that they'd characterize primarily as "frustrating and discouraging." As Barrie Peterson pointed out, "I try not to define a season as discouraging or frustrating when we have advanced to the state meet! [Advancing to state] automatically makes the season worthwhile!" Sam Rasmussen also prefers not to think about a season in those terms. A coach should take control of defining success according to his or her values; if success depends on a positive event cancelling out negative events, "you need to change the way you coach."

Steve Kearney never simplified success down to one particular race. He didn't even narrow it down to a single season. Kearney explained, "I don't think we had any state meets that I would classify as terrible. High school kids are always improving year-to-year, and any season that seems successful has at least three leading into it." Kearney understands that the state meet is just a snapshot, a dot on a timeline. To him, it would be unwise to make overarching judgments about success or failure based on the results of one single performance.

We consider every coach in our study to be highly successful. That is, after all, why we included them in this book. Ironically, the metrics we used when we labeled them 'successful' and included them in this study are overwhelmingly not the same metrics that they use when they evaluate their own success. In defining success outside of measurable wins and losses, the coaches display respect for sportsmanship and the spirit of competition. Weinheimer's team motto is "Making our team very tough to beat," a phrase that hints at respect for the toughness of competitors and the purity of fair sport. Chuck Koeppen, after 23 team state championships as a head coach, defines success as follows: "A great team must have a special chemistry, a tremendous bond of togetherness, and actually care about one another. If a coach can get that out of his or her team...that is SUCCESS!"

Enduring Wisdom

CHAPTER 10: FACING FAILURE

*"I consider everything for myself as well as the
athletes to be growth opportunities. With that in
mind, it is hard to call anything a failure."*
- Steve Kearney

Everybody fails. When asked, each coach could point to a vivid example of having fallen short of hopes and expectations. They didn't hide their frustration over their past shortcomings. What made these coaches successful in the end was that they turned that so-called failure into a growth opportunity.

The Response is What Matters

Scott Lidskin called his team's 2000 season a "massive failure." With 40% of the team injured at some point during that season, they never raced as well as they could have. But from another perspective, that "failure" was a pivotal step toward success. "That season was *hugely* important in my development. We completely overhauled our training and began to incorporate swimming into the training regimen," he explained. Lidskin's team did not qualify for the state meet that year or the next, but the year 2000 was a turning point in how he approached training. The adjustments that he made paid huge dividends for the next group of runners to come through his program, and his teams would go on to win three consecutive state titles in 2005, 2006, and 2007.

The enduring effect of failure depends on the way a coach responds to it. For Eric Kellison, as for Lidskin, that meant taking personal responsibility. Kellison talked about "owning" the negative outcome as a coach, rather than blaming the runners. Sure, there were things the athletes could have done better, but Kellison chose to look instead at himself. "More times than not, I blamed myself...I screwed up the training," he recalled. But he didn't wallow. Instead, he focused on what he could change. "Best thing to do is review your training, talk with great coaches, and reevaluate what you are doing. I reevaluated the entire program, from workouts and races to diet, rest, etc. There is always something I could have done better."

Looking for ways to "do better" is how Chuck Koeppen developed Carmel's winning program. In 1974, an ambitious young Koeppen was sure that his team could win their first state championship. They'd placed fifth the year before, and most runners would be returning. After a great summer of training, things looked promising. "We were good, and we were blowing people away." But as the season progressed, they saw injuries and burn-out. "Other teams were catching up to us. We finished a disappointing 11th place in the State. Those kids deserved to win, but I trained them too hard." Koeppen saw his mistakes and made changes to his training program. "I learned a lot from that season. Like the turtle and the hare, you have to pace yourself....I was too much in a hurry, and it cost us." Two years later (1976) he won his first state title. Over the next 32 years he would go on to win 22 more.

Mike Prow's 2004 team thought they might win state, but instead they experienced disappointment, thanks to unbelievably steady 30-40 mile-per-hour winds, with gusts much higher. Prow explained, "There was *terrible* wind, but we went out really hard anyway, our seven probably blocking the wind for everyone. And we finished 19th, second to last." Prow and his athletes reflected on their disappointment and responded with a new plan the next year. His 2005 team pulled off one of the most interesting team strategies Prow had ever witnessed at the state meet. At around 1000 meters into the race, the entire pack of 7 Valparaiso runners were together near the very back of the field. As the race developed, everyone could see the team moving up together methodically, and they passed runners at a seemingly exponential rate as they neared the finish line. They finished in second place, and if they'd had another 100 meters they very well might have won. This turnaround wasn't merely about achieving a higher place at the state meet; it was about learning to strategize.

The coaches' stories displayed a pattern: Coaches pointed out mistakes they made early in their careers, owned the results, reflected on their practice, and made positive changes. In every instance we saw that the coach's response was far more important to overall development than the actual mistakes that had been made. Their failures were never permanent; rather, they were opportunities to learn and grow.

The Growth Mindset

The way Lidskin, Kellison, Koeppen, and Prow responded to setbacks is not quite as simple as choosing to "look on the bright side" and persevere. In order to really learn from failure, they had to look their imperfections square in the face, matter-of-factly, without shame. They were unafraid to try new training methods because they had what Dr. Carol Dweck, a psychology professor at Stanford University, calls a "growth mindset." Rather than believing that their abilities are fixed, people with a growth mindset believe they can always learn more. Instead of shrinking back from challenges for fear of proving their inadequacy, growth-minded people take risks in order to learn as they go. They are intrinsically motivated to improve themselves rather than extrinsically pressured to prove themselves. So instead of worrying about what others think, they address their weaknesses and work on them without needing to be prodded. We gave our coaches a Carol Dweck-inspired quiz to assess whether they had a "growth mindset" or a "fixed mindset." As you can see in the table at the end of this chapter, they were, on average, almost four times as likely to agree with growth mindset statements as with fixed.

In her best-selling book *Mindset: The New Psychology of Success (2006)*, Dweck includes a chapter specifically for parents, teachers and coaches about developing a child's growth mindset. She noticed that "The great teachers believe in the growth of the intellect and talent, and they are fascinated with the process of learning" (p. 194). When kids think their talent or ability is a fixed trait, then failing is a problem that cannot be overcome and should be avoided. But when kids believe that their response to failure is more important than the failure itself, they challenge themselves and they grow. To this end, great coaches cultivate a growth mindset, not only in themselves, but also in their athletes. For example, Rick Weinheimer strategically designed his entire training program to embrace the growth mindset, and he coined a team catchphrase: "Hard work, given time, beats talent"—a phrase we heard from Brad Peterson as well. Erhard Bell likewise tells his athletes that failure is only "an endeavor temporarily off-track."

Having a growth mindset doesn't mean you don't acknowledge your disappointment. Sometimes it is appropriate to be upset. In 2006, Barrie Peterson's final year of coaching before retiring, his team unexpectedly failed to advance out of semi-state, missing the coveted position by just one place. So many of Peterson's former athletes were present that day, prepared to see him go out with a bang. He was "at a loss for words," which is uncharacteristic of him. But despite the team's disappointment, two individuals made it to state, coached by a dynamic Barrie Peterson for one more week. Responding to failure with a growth mindset doesn't mean Peterson brushed aside the failure. But it meant the failure did not define him or his team, it did not keep him from moving on to the next challenge, and it did not detract from his legacy of success.

Letting Kids Fail

The coaches had turned their own failures into growth opportunities, so we wondered what they thought about using failure as a coaching strategy. We asked a loaded question: "Have you ever intentionally let an athlete fail when you could have intervened, in order to use failure as a learning tool?"

While acknowledging failure's natural role in growth, the coaches answered us with a resounding NO! The athletes' experience should always be positive, they said, and artificially creating failure doesn't square with that belief. Failure is bound to happen on its own. Erhard Bell said, "I have never allowed an athlete to intentionally fail, since I am always about being positive in one's approach to running."

Young athletes must believe their coach is ultimately on their side, even when they disagree. Karen DeVries saw herself not as an objective observer, but as an active participant in her team's struggles. She explained, "As a coach I tried turning any negative experience into something positive. I was the one with experience, the girls were not. I could get them thinking positively just by the way I approached things. I would never allow an athlete to 'fail' if the result would be negative and hard for that athlete to emotionally recover from." DeVries didn't shield her runners from struggle, and she was sometimes tough on them, but she always kept in mind that the psyche of her athletes was less developed and more fragile than her own.

Resistance to "letting them fail" doesn't mean a coach shelters athletes from the experience when it happens. Steve Lewark acknowledged that many athletes only learn some lessons, like racing strategy, the hard way. He explained, "Most young runners come into the program not knowing how to race properly (at least how I believe is proper). Sometimes it takes going out hard and dying a few times before they realize that what I am telling them is best. But you have to let them learn that on their own." Lewark was giving them instruction and pulling for them all along, but he knew the learning would take time and plenty of mistakes. Tim Ray also emphasizes to his runners that failure is inevitable, but that "it's what you take from that failure that you use to become a better runner or person." He quoted author Jeff Goins: "[F]ailure means I'm not dead. When I die and go to heaven, things will be perfect. Until then, I will be surrounded by imperfection, especially my own. The good news in this is that it means I'm not dead" (Goins).

Addressing Fear of Failure

Despite the coaches' healthy approach to growing through setbacks, some athletes are gripped by a debilitating fear of failure. Toeing the line of the state championship race can be a daunting proposition for them. An entire season, or even an entire high school career, seems to boil down to one race. In addressing this kind of fear, the coaches tailor their approach to each specific athlete. Yet they shared some general advice that has worked for them:

1. Find the root cause.

Scott Lidskin explained, "There are so many techniques to use to overcome fear. The first step is to find out what the athlete is afraid of and then come up with a strategy to combat that. Everyone is afraid to a certain extent, and once the athlete realizes this, he or she can improve." Though fear may look similar in different athletes, its cause is often rooted in personal experience. It's important to listen to the athlete's perception and to consider the athlete's background and life circumstances. When Josh Fletcher spends most of his coaching time "reaching each athlete," he is positioning himself as someone who can help individual athletes reflect, confront vulnerabilities, and move forward. In Fletcher's words, "Every athlete is different and requires a different key to unlock their potential."

2. Downplay the outcome.

Mark Ellington and Zach Raber talked about downplaying the outcome and focusing on the process instead. Mark Ellington told us, "My approach is to eliminate the end results. Most athletes are not going to be presented with fear during workout days, but the idea is to build confidence in small segments. Once you build that in practice, then you set the same kind of plan for race day." Zach Raber remembers an effective strategy that he used for an athlete who was prone to this fear of failure. He intended to "remove as much negative pressure regarding winning as possible. We focused on her process goals instead of her outcome goals." Ellington and Raber removed negative pressure by setting everyday goals that pertained to training instead of discussing race goals. Instead of letting a single race become the focus, they made smaller, actionable goals for workouts, and celebrated successes throughout the process. They were confident that a consistent approach to getting better every day would lead to success in the end.

3. Focus on the team, not the individual.

Mike Prow explained that when the weight of a goal is shared among a team, everyone's shoulders feel a little bit lighter. Sam Rasmussen shared a similar idea. "Give your best where you can, you can't do any more. Focus on what you can control. Be able to turn to your teammates and say to each of them, 'I did the best that I could.'" The shared accountability mitigates individual pressure and diffuses it out to all members of the team.

4. Don't sugarcoat the problem.

Downplaying the outcome and focusing on the team shouldn't translate into pretending fear isn't a problem that must be addressed. Josh Fletcher had to implement a bit of tough love in order to help one of his athletes overcome debilitating fear. Fletcher said, "I had a girl in track who always cried, I mean *sobbed*, before races. I had finally had enough when her actions started negatively affecting the other girls on our team. I told her that if she cried before a race again I was not going to let her compete that day. The next time she exercised her fear-of-failure crying episode, I told her to get off the track and she didn't run. It cost our team points, and she felt horrible about it, and that caused more crying." She had been focused only on herself, which had amplified her fears. By showing her how her fear was affecting the team, Fletcher was pointing out the runners' interconnectedness. "The next opportunity she had to race, miraculously, there were no tears. She didn't cry before a race the remainder of her track career. To this day she still thanks me for helping her overcome her fear of failure."

5. Embrace positive reinforcement.

Late in Joe Brooks' career, a new runner moved in from across the country. "He was a sophomore who was off-the-charts smart. He was very quiet and did not seem to make friends easily. He was, however, a talented runner. We went to the Culver Invitational where they have a frosh/soph race. Carmel usually wins this race every year. That year we had 5 really good freshmen and sophomores. With 1K to go in the race, this new runner was running great, and as he passed by me during that last K, I was screaming my head off for him to get one more runner, because we had a chance to finally win this race. As he runs by me he yells, 'I don't care.' He slowed down and barely jogged to the line, and we lost by 1 point to Carmel. I realized then that this was his defense mechanism because he was afraid to fail. My first knee-jerk reaction was to kill him. However, I found that he did not respond to words that put pressure on him. He responded to positive reinforcement like 'you look great,' 'you look strong,' 'you da man.'" Brooks individualized his approach to maximize the young man's talent. "As a senior he was in our top 7 on a state championship team."

The coaches took a quiz on www.mindsetonline.com. It consisted of sixteen statements, eight that conveyed a growth mindset and eight that conveyed a fixed mindset. For each statement, they either agreed or disagreed. The table below shows how many growth mindset statements (of 8) each coach agreed with and how many fixed mindset statements (of 8) each coach agreed with. Coaches could have agreed with all 16 statements or disagreed with all 16 statements, the purpose of the quiz is to identify which of the two mindsets they agree with more often. The third column shows the difference for each coach, with a positive number indicating a stronger growth mindset and a negative number indicating a stronger fixed mindset. You can see in the table that only one coach had a negative difference (and only -1 at that), three had a neutral difference (score of 0), and the rest had a positive growth mindset. It is clear that this group of coaches has a strong collective leaning toward a growth mindset.

COACH	GROWTH	FIXED	Difference
Koeppen	4	0	+4
Fletcher	7	2	+5
Prow	8	0	+8
Rasmussen	8	1	+7
Ellington	8	0	+8
Bell	4	4	0
Lidskin	4	4	0
Ray	5	2	+3
Kellison	8	8	0
DeVries	8	1	+7
Lewark	8	0	+8
Raber	8	1	+7
Altevogt	5	3	+2
Brad Peterson	2	3	-1
Brooks	8	0	+8
Weinheimer	8	0	+8
Barrie Peterson	7	1	+6
Kearney	8	0	+6
AVERAGES	**6.6**	**1.7**	**+4.8**

Chapter 11: Planning the Training

"Use the science of our sport to set up a plan of workouts for the season. However, learn to be flexible. The plan should not be written in stone."
- Rick Stover

"The schedule can be a good plan, but you have to be flexible when something creates a demand for change."
- Mark Ellington

Thus far we have observed our coaches' leadership traits. Chapters 11 through 17 will focus on these coaches as trainers of athletes. Chapters 12 through 17 will explore training in more specific detail, but first let's seek to understand how our coaches approach the big picture of distance training. Coaches are master planners. Each week and each workout is scheduled with purpose. We asked them to describe how they plan their athletes' training, and three themes emerged:

1. Tailor Your Training to Your Team

One might presume that a coach who has succeeded at the highest level has figured out a blueprint that can be applied successfully to each new team. On the contrary, we observed overwhelmingly that coaches tailor their training plan specifically to each year's team. Every season is a new chapter.

Sam Rasmussen sat down at the beginning of each cross country season and asked himself some questions: "What are strengths and weaknesses of my runners? What are strengths and weaknesses of our team? What are strengths and weaknesses of our schedule?" Rasmussen's 1985 Valparaiso team won the state meet with 79 points, and the following year they returned five varsity runners, a strong nucleus of the team. But even then, Rasmussen began the 1986 season with a fresh approach. They had graduated two of their top scorers, and Rasmussen wasn't taking it for granted that their needs were the same. He asked himself the same questions about this new team and tailored the training plan accordingly. In 1986, all five of Valparaiso's returning runners placed higher at the state meet than the previous year, and they won again, this time with an even lower score of 66 points.

Many coaches echoed this approach, altering their training plans each year. Mike Prow said, "Creating the season plan depends on the caliber of runners that you have." For Scott Lidskin, changing training from year to year "depends on the makeup of our team." Each team is different, and the plan that worked for last year's team might not work again this year. Joe Brooks noted the specific needs of young teams versus veteran teams. "I had [veteran teams] do more reps for a particular workout. If I had a young team, then they might not do quite as much as previous years." Zach Raber said that great coaches "find the plan that's best for each athlete and implement it in the context of the team environment."

Not only do coaches tailor their overall training plans to each team, but they also tailor training specifically to each athlete. Karen DeVries determined the training season by "the type of summer the girls had, the goal of the season, along with individual goals. Each year is different." Eric Kellison agreed. "It is important to realize what type of team you have and develop what works best for the individuals and the team," he said. Brad Peterson told us, "I individualize every single season and every single kid." It sounds like a lot of work (and it is), but I (Derek) coached with Brad from 2004-2006 at Concordia Lutheran HS, and I can assure you that he is not exaggerating. Every day he brought a specific workout plan and specific goal times for each athlete. For weekly mileage goals, each athlete had an individualized plan. Among top coaches, Peterson's meticulous approach is quite common. Organizing goals and results on spreadsheets is a near-daily activity, not one reserved for meets.

At Carmel HS, Colin Altevogt's varsity boys might each run very different workouts late in the season. "We've had some varsity guys in the past who prefer to continue their long runs and threshold runs up until the state meet. If that works for them, it works for me." It is not unusual to observe an October practice at Carmel where varsity athletes are doing entirely separate workouts, based on what each runner needs most.

Altevogt and others who individualize training plans are not making things up off the cuff or letting runners do whatever they want. Instead, they possess a dual understanding: a clear knowledge of training physiology and an equally clear knowledge of the athletes they coach. Instead of following a strict blueprint for success, they craft a plan they can adapt continually.

2. Plan Forward or Backward

Those adaptable plans often take the form of a season-long schedule. Being in the same state, with the same general racing schedule, you might expect their planning to be similar. But we found two main planning approaches: forward and backward. Some look at Day 1 and start building a training schedule forward from there, while others look at the state meet and plan backwards from there. In all, ten coaches considered themselves to be backward planners, and seven coaches considered themselves to be forward planners.

Forward Planners

The forward planners gave two compelling reasons for why they start on Day 1 and plan forward. First, our coaches talked about the vital importance of a solid aerobic base of mileage. Colin Altevogt explained, "I tend to plan from the start of the season and go from there. Because of the importance of aerobic strength in cross country, I think maximizing our time in this regard is vital. I think it's more important to give plenty of time for 'base' for each athlete." Similarly, even though everything Josh Fletcher's team does is "geared towards the state finals," he is a forward planner because "it is more important to have 10-12 weeks of completely aerobic training before moving forward to other types of training to maximize an athlete's state meet performance." Rick Weinheimer also plans forward, looking first at his runners' training levels on day 1 and building from there. "The more they do during the summer, the more quickly they can progress," he said. These coaches realize that if they shortchange the base phase of training, then all other types of training they do later in the season will be less effective. There simply is no shortcut to strong aerobic fitness. That realization led these coaches to think forward in how they plan training, focusing first on establishing a solid base of mileage. Eric Kellison summarized this mindset: "Make huge deposits early for future withdrawals."

There is a second reason that coaches describe themselves as forward planners: You never really know how a season is going to unfold. Chuck Koeppen said, "Usually, we would just work from the start of the season. This was due to the 'unknowns' that existed prior to the season." Barrie Peterson said something very similar, "I usually look at the start of the season and plan forward from there because so much can happen throughout the season to do it any other way! There are certain check points along the way (key meets, important workouts, etc.) that help to keep me on point and allow for flexibility in meet planning and workouts." Coaches like Koeppen and Peterson felt that training with a forward mindset allowed them the flexibility to respond to inevitable unknown factors later in the season. The seven forward planners were Colin Altevogt, Josh Fletcher, Eric Kellison, Chuck Koeppen, Barrie Peterson, Mike Prow, and Rick Weinheimer.

Backward Planners

The backward planners had equally compelling reasons for starting their training plans at the end of the season and working backward. Karen DeVries explained, "I look at the state meet and plan backwards. I do this because I know what condition I want to see the team in at certain points of the season, which dictates what workouts are needed to get those results. Everything we do is geared for the state meet."

Tim Ray agreed, saying, "We take a look at where we want to be at our best, then we do work backwards from there. I think it is easier to work backwards from where you want to end. We can adjust where we need to and move things around when necessary." Mark Ellington also plans backward "because we want to keep the goal in mind, and it's easier to have what you really want late in the season by making adjustments 12, 8, or even 4 weeks earlier in the schedule." The backward planners found it easier to adjust their training plan when they kept their focus on the final target, which for all our coaches was the state cross country meet. The ten backward planners were Erhard Bell, Joe Brooks, Karen DeVries, Mark Ellington, Steve Kearney, Steve Lewark, Brad Peterson, Zach Raber, Sam Rasmussen, and Tim Ray.

Both forward and backward planners consistently emphasized the importance of flexibility and being able to adjust their plans as they go. The difference was in how they created that flexibility in their overall training plans.

3. Evaluate as You Go

In implementing their flexible plans, the real question became one of discernment: When does a coach need to change the plan? Most coaches develop a series of training "phases" that function as a framework for writing their training plan, typically starting with a base mileage phase, then incorporating anaerobic threshold training and eventually interval training. In both year-to-year adjustments and adaptations within a given season, knowing when to tweak the plan or adjust a phase was vital. It takes a practiced eye, but our coaches looked for signs of fatigue, benchmarks for improvement, and changes in the achievability of their goals as they continually evaluated the plan.

Our coaches stood ready to adjust their plans to ensure adequate recovery and avoid overtraining. Zach Raber's best indicator was "seeing how the athletes react to the process. If they are extremely tired, we need to adjust. If they are racing poorly in consecutive weeks, we adjust. If we talk to them and they are just not feeling right, we adjust." Steve Kearney relied on "watching for dead legs—not being able to respond late in races." Chuck Koeppen explained, "You just have to watch your runners and determine if they are progressing or not. Sometimes they may just be 'dead' due to overtraining. There is a fine line between training to be your very best and getting injured or becoming overly fatigued."

Brad Peterson challenged coaches not to get locked into a weekly schedule in which you always do specific workouts on specific days, at the expense of athletes' recovery. "Perhaps you need to really adjust your Thursday and not do as much. Push that workout to Wednesday. Young kids probably need more confidence-boost races, so they may need to feel fresher for meets than the veterans." Moving Thursday workouts to Wednesday gives an extra recovery day before a Saturday meet. Steve Lewark agreed. "This is where the art of coaching comes in. If you know your runners, you can tell if they are recovering from races and from workouts. If not, you either reduce the mileage and/or cut back on the number of reps." Success in long distance running requires hard training, but great coaches strive to identify when athletes are training too much.

Another way coaches evaluate their plans is through benchmarks for improvement. If athletes don't improve throughout the season, something needs to change. Erhard Bell noted that, in addition to adjusting for weather conditions, he adjusts workout sessions "based on the progress (or lack thereof) of the team [and] the responses of the athletes ... Flexibility is crucial with the training." Many coaches use specific meets each year to check their teams' progress. For Eric Kellison, it was the FlashRock Invitational. Josh Fletcher said, "I use New Prairie and Conference weekends to evaluate our mid-season progress in hopes of making small changes to help our cause." Barrie Peterson kept meticulous records of workout and meet results every year so that he could easily compare team and individual meet and workout results. "Looking for improvement in several benchmark workouts was a key to our success or lack thereof," he said.

Variables that affect training are changing all the time. Tim Ray explained how sometimes the goals of a team or an athlete change, and training changes to reflect that. "If the goal seems to have changed within the season, then we will adjust so that we have the best opportunity to reach that goal." We began this chapter with Sam Rasmussen as he sat crafting a plan for his 1986 team, looking for strengths and weaknesses that had changed since the previous year. Yet Rasmussen didn't stop questioning himself after he'd written the plan. "Even though I would write workouts for the entire season, I would review them at the end of each week. There was never a week where I did not readjust the workout that was planned," he said. Those adjustments were crucial to his back-to-back state championships in 1985 and 1986.

In planning, coaches follow three general principles: One, they change their plans every year, tailoring each year's schedule to that specific team. Two, whether they are forward or backward planners, they all purposely build flexibility into their training plans so they can adjust them throughout the season. Three, they constantly evaluate as they go. Karen DeVries calls constant evaluation "part of the coaching process," and Scott Lidskin pointed out that "if you don't change, you will eventually fail." He adjusts his plan every year regardless of results. Great coaches understand the variables that affect training and prepare to adapt when those variables change.

Chapter 12: Peaking at the Right Time

"There are no secrets to peaking."
- Barrie Peterson

Distance runners have long been preoccupied with *peaking*, a massive, meaning-of-the-universe concept for many cross country coaches. Known as *periodization* in scientific circles, peaking means maximizing your performance at a targeted point in your training cycle by systematically planning various phases of training. In other words, peaking means training to run your best races at the end of the season. Master the art of peaking, the thinking goes, and every practice leads flawlessly to that perfect final race.

The experts we feature have collectively won dozens and dozens of cross country state championships, so if anyone could say how to peak at the right time, it would be these coaches. Yet they seemed as unsure as anyone. No coach presented a reproducible plan for peaking runners correctly. In fact, some were utterly unconcerned with the question of peaking at all.

Tim Ray said modestly, "I really don't know any secrets to peaking." Chuck Koeppen (after 22 team state titles in cross country) believes that peaking "is somewhat of an educated guess." Steve Lewark went as far as saying, "I am not a big fan of peaking in cross country." It's not that peaking is a hoax or a waste of time but that it is elusive. No precise plan ensures all your athletes will run their best race on a specific calendar date. There is no big secret. But there are plenty of little secrets. Here are a few of our coaches' insights on peaking.

Make Peaking Mental

"Myth number one is physically peaking itself," Scott Lidskin told us. "We don't think it is possible for a coach to honestly tell an athlete that we can guarantee their success on a given day. We do, however, strongly believe in a mental peaking." Traditionally, runners have thought of peaking in physiological terms: your aerobic fitness and running economy improve until you're at your best, just in time for the state meet. Yet most of the coaches to whom we spoke believe peaking is more mental than physical. Erhard Bell finds peaking to be "mainly a mental issue versus pure physiology." Tim Ray agrees that "more than anything, it is psychological."

Of course the mental is deeply rooted in the physical. Karen DeVries cautioned against getting hung up on the details of physical peaking and overthinking it. "The over-guiding principle is preparation equals motivation equals confidence. To be ready psychologically, you first need to prepare physically. The more physically ready, the more mentally ready your team will be." DeVries' athletes ran their best races at the end of the season because they were confident in their training. The physical preparation was important to DeVries not only because it produced physical fitness but primarily because it produced mental fitness.

Zach Raber admitted that chasing a physical peak is incredibly difficult. Like DeVries, he prefers to focus on the mental side of the equation. "Instead of changing a bunch of plans in regards to training," he told us, "I try to work more on their confidence." Mike Prow echoed that thought. He says the key to peaking is "believing in their coach and the program." By committing their energy to developing athletes' confidence and mental fitness, these coaches turn physical fitness into a means to that end, rather than an end in itself. When mental peaking is the goal, physical peaking is often a welcome by-product, which leads to more consistent results.

Maintain Mileage Volume

Since mental peaking depends so greatly on physical preparation, our coaches do stick to some principles of physical training to produce results and confidence for the end of the season. Have you ever heard a coach, after a strong team performance at a September invitational, say, "Just wait until we taper, then we'll really run fast!"? Most of our championship coaches would cringe hearing those words. The single biggest mistake coaches make late in the cross country season is to cut back too much on weekly mileage volume.

"I think tapering is overrated and can backfire," Brad Peterson told us. Conventional wisdom says that cutting volume in favor of short, fast intervals late in the season preserves runners' energy and helps them run their fastest come tournament time. Peterson disagrees. "That's the opposite of how you should think. Keep doing the strength-based stuff, as it is synonymous with speed." This was a lesson that Joe Brooks learned early in his career. "Some myths I experienced as a coach were to cut way back on workout efforts, cut way back on weekly mileage and cut out morning practices. This was supposed to make runners peak at the right time. I found that you do need to have your runners feel fresh, but drastic changes were not productive. When we did drastic changes in our weekly routine it threw our team in the wrong direction."

107

Several coaches admitted that they do cut volume at the end of the season, but only very subtly. Eric Kellison's team backed off their base volume twice each season, "once at a mid-season meet and then at Semi-state. We backed off mornings and then mileage and wham! Huge races!" Steve Lewark said he would cut back by about 10-15%, but only the week of the state meet. Colin Altevogt and Steve Kearney agreed. Their athletes cut back by about 10-20% just for the state meet week. Altevogt really prefers to stay closer to 10%.

Keep in mind that 10-20% is not a large decrease. An athlete running 50 miles per week throughout the season would still run 40-45 miles for the state meet week. None of these coaches made drastic cuts in mileage. And they only talked about backing off volume immediately before a race. The decrease in volume was not stretched out over multiple weeks.

Maintain Intensity in Hard Workouts

If cutting too much volume is the number one mistake that coaches make late in the season, then cutting intensity is mistake number two. Barrie Peterson cuts volume slightly at the end of the season, but he is very clear that "you must keep the intensity for hard workouts right on up to the state meet." The most intense workouts that his athletes ran each season were in October. Logically, that makes sense; if your training plan has your athletes at their highest fitness in October, then their workouts should reflect that.

Rick Weinheimer is known for maintaining high workout intensity right up until the state meet. A fellow coach once asked him to explain his team's state-week workouts. Weinheimer shared how intense their workouts are that final week, and the other coach, bordering on disbelief, admitted that he could never ask so much of his own team. He simply could not fathom that a coach would still be so intense in the final days preceding the state meet. Weinheimer says, "The 'secret' is not a secret. *Keep* their oxygen delivery systems at maximum by continuing the same volume and effort during aerobic training, and *allow* the glycogen to refill."

Flexibility, which our coaches build into their big-picture training programs, should not compromise the intensity of workouts during tournament time. Mark Ellington stressed the importance of sticking to the plan when it comes to intensity. "We keep our training very consistent. The girls have a general expectation of how the week will look, and we stick to it. Prior to semi-state or state, we might reduce the volume of the long run by a mile or two and we might do one less repeat. We really don't change the program much." Their volume decreases slightly, but they do not back off the intensity.

Keep the Routine, Amplify the Details

To maximize performance in the postseason, coaches adhered to a sort of dualism: they strove to keep things routine while at the same time magnifying the details that may otherwise have been overlooked. Josh Fletcher said, "I try to do a really good job at all the small things during the last five weeks. Things like boys shaving their legs, athletes not eating sugar, more sleep, better overall nutrition, guest speakers at practice, a team banquet, special tournament shirts, new or different uniforms, community service projects, and reminders about tradition. Basically, I'm trying to create the most supportive and inspirational climate I can." Note that Fletcher is emphasizing these details during the last five weeks of the season, not just the final week. Instead of reaching for something special during the last week of the season, Fletcher is sustaining and perfecting what is already in place. Sam Rasmussen recalled that late in the season his team "talked about...what we meant to each other." Spotlighting supportive relationships builds confidence, and details like sleep and nutrition minimize the risk of a late-season illness or injury, at a time when the stakes are high and the physical training has mostly been done.

Yet they amplify these details within a framework of calm and routine. While pressing upon his athletes to "get a little more rest and stay off their feet as much as possible," Sam Rasmussen cautioned his athletes not to change their diets or any other routine details right before big races. Joe Brooks advised, "If you have been doing morning practices, don't completely stop them." Coaches hope to foster both mental and physical peaking by keeping routines and rituals in place, refocusing the athletes on their collective goals, and paying special attention to every small detail that could give them a postseason advantage.

Chapter 13: Mileage

"I've tried to work on increasing mileage for my athletes, men and women, over the course of their 4-year careers."
- Zach Raber

Mileage is the heart of distance training. Our sport's culture rewards meticulous measuring and record-keeping, and one of the most basic measurements is also a great source of pride for many runners: their mileage. Runners love measuring mileage because of its straightforward simplicity: it seems to prove there is no secret shortcut to fitness. Mileage also provides one of the easiest ways to brag to non-runners, many of whom are unfamiliar with other components of our sport but know how long a mile is. Most runners consider "mileage" to be the number of miles run in a given week, so in this chapter any mention of mileage will refer to weekly measures. When our coaches explained their thoughts on mileage, we observed five key points.

Mileage Has Decreased in Recent Decades

High mileage can take on a sort of prestige, and non-runners often ask runners, "How many miles per week do you run?" (along with the ever-popular "What's your mile time?" and "Have you ever run a marathon?"). Perhaps this fixation on mileage is helped along by the rising popularity of the ultra-marathon niche. But even in the relatively short distance of high school races (up to 5K in Indiana), runners seem to measure each other's true commitment by the number of miles run per week.

The prestige of high mileage is something of a holdover from an earlier age. During the running boom of the 1960s and 70s, when the infamous Gerry

Lindgren was putting in 200-mile weeks, the predominant attitude toward training seemed to be that more is always better. Some longtime coaches in our group emphasized high mileage back then. Barrie Peterson, who began coaching in 1966, once had his athletes running up to 100 miles weekly. Sam Rasmussen, who coached from 1974 to 1988, said his Valparaiso runners sometimes ran "well over a hundred miles per week." High schoolers run far fewer miles now than they did in the 1970s. The highest number from our current coaches was 70-75, and most of them maxed out around 50-60 miles per week for their top runners. Over the past forty years, the definition of "high mileage" for boys' teams in Indiana has decreased from 100 miles per week to 70 miles per week. (Girls' mileage trends are harder to pinpoint over time because girls' cross country did not begin in Indiana until 1981, and girls' races increased from 4K to 5K as recently as ten years ago.)

Those who coached for decades witnessed this change and evolved with the times. Early on, Rasmussen had been driven by the truth that there is no substitute for working hard to achieve your best, but by 1984 he had realized that "your best cannot be attained unless you are rested to give your best." Peterson also says now that the "more is better" mentality is a big mistake. In his early years, his emphasis on mileage kept him from adjusting his training to an athlete's specific needs. "Back in the high mileage craze of the late '60s and early '70s, most of my athletes pretty much ran the same mileage and the same workouts, maxing out at 100 miles per week. I finally got smart and realized the importance of individualizing workouts, from total mileage to number of reps. During the final years of my time at Northrop, our freshmen ran 30-45 miles per week and seniors ranged from 45 to 70 miles per week."

Downplaying Mileage

One longtime coach who bucked the high mileage trend was Chuck Koeppen, who began coaching in 1968 at Daleville HS and then moved to Wapahani HS before beginning at Carmel in 1972. When hopeful young coaches ask Chuck Koeppen about mileage, they sometimes have a hard time accepting his answer. "While I was at Carmel," Koeppen said, "we were given credit for running more mileage than we actually ran. I am not sure why this was, but our guys actually averaged 50+ miles per week, and our girls somewhere in the low 40s." Koeppen spoke at coaching clinics and explained his training program, but some people assumed that they *must* have been doing far greater mileage than he would divulge.

Similarly, Eric Kellison rejected the high mileage philosophy. He capped boys off around 50 miles per week, and often his athletes ran less than that. He advised, "Do not run kids more than that [50 miles]. Aaron Fisher ran 15:25 [for a 5k] at 35 miles per week, same with Jason Crist." People who talked to Kellison found it difficult to believe that an athlete the caliber of Aaron Fisher could win three consecutive state titles running only 35 miles per week.

Scott Lidskin downplayed the importance of high mileage too. "Mileage is not a number that we talk about with our athletes, and we don't even talk about it too much as a coaching staff. We talk about the duration of the long run and the volume of threshold and VO2 work." For Lidskin, the number of miles that an athlete runs each week is tertiary at best. In his mind, there are far more important metrics to look at.

Mileage Varies

The more recent drop in mileage should not be seen as a wholesale rejection of its importance, but instead as a tempering. Coaches know there's no substitute for time spent running, but more of them now value a balance between work and rest, and they try to personalize training for their athletes. When asked their teams' mileage, every coach gave a "well, that depends" sort of qualifier. Most don't have a specific number, but instead share a wide range into which most of their athletes fall – a mileage bell curve. No pun intended, but Erhard Bell was one who shared a fairly large mileage range. "We will vary from 20 to 50 miles per week running 6 days a week and usually taking off Sundays." Thirty miles is a significant difference from the bottom to the top. Joe Brooks, who began coaching in 1979 on the tail end of the high mileage craze, shared a range on the higher end for our group, but still within what most contemporary coaches would consider reasonable: "During the last few weeks of the summer and the first month of the season my top runners averaged 60-75 miles a week."

Scott Lidskin varies mileage based on age, talent, and "durability." Some runners have a particular body type or rough running form that make them more injury prone, while others have a body type and a smoother running form that help them to be very durable. Tim Ray pointed out that this variation also changes from year to year, as athletes develop. "The amount of mileage is different per runner and season. There are weeks within a season in which some of our runners have reached 70 to 75, and other seasons the top runner was at 40. I think it depends on experience and where each athlete is within the concept of the training program." Additionally, with the online availability of diverse training methods, the mentality of fitness-savvy parents can also affect an athlete's mileage.

Later in this chapter you'll see some statistics and percentages from our coaches' responses. But keep in mind that there is no simple answer. Almost all our coaches clearly stated that mileage varies among athletes.

Increases Are Gradual and Cautious

It may seem obvious that freshmen and other first-year runners should run fewer miles than older runners. Even during Sam Rasmussen's 100-mile weeks, he was very careful with freshmen. "With younger runners we were trying to get them interested in running, trying to whet their appetite to the fun and accomplishment of running. Your job is to make them love the sport. Too much too soon will just drive them away."

A dilemma arises when a particularly talented freshman joins the team and seems to be able to handle any workout that a coach puts before them. In this scenario it becomes an easy trap for a coach to assign too many miles, mistaking natural talent for a physical ability to handle rapid increases in mileage. In cases like this, Brad Peterson relies on his knowledge of the runner's background. He gets familiar with every runner's history when they come into his program. "You have to know their experience as a runner from grade school," he says. Mike Prow errs on the side of caution during the early base training period, even with talented young runners. "Our freshmen only do 30-40 minutes [daily] of running during the week over the summer, except a long run of 50-70 minutes on Saturday."

115

If you train freshmen carefully, you can create a mileage baseline from which to increase mileage gradually over four years. Zach Raber worked to improve each athlete's mileage gradually over four years—an approach he has continued in his current position at the collegiate level. Josh Fletcher starts his runners off low and increases each year. "I expect all freshmen to run around 30 miles per week and add 10 miles per week each year in high school." Fletcher's senior runners commonly run 60 miles per week. That might seem like a high number, but it has been the result of incremental increases over time. Erhard Bell recommends not increasing an athlete's weekly mileage by more than 5 miles at a time, and only when the runner has clearly demonstrated in training a physical readiness for the increase.

Mileage Differences Between Genders

People commonly assume that girls should run fewer miles than boys. In fact, until 2006, high school girls' cross country races in Indiana were only 4 kilometers long, while boys raced 5k. Some of our coaches described girls as more "injury prone" than boys, reasoning that their mileage should be limited. Science generally agrees that girls are often at greater risk for sports injuries (Schmerling, 2015).

However, many coaches expressed that mileage numbers should be much closer than conventional wisdom might indicate. Sam Rasmussen said that the "difference in mileage between boys and girls is probably not as much as people think." Erhard Bell believes that gender is "not as important as their overall experience with running when determining their weekly miles." Josh Fletcher and Steve Lewark coach both boys and girls, and neither considers gender to be a major factor when assigning mileage values. Fletcher typically decides weekly mileage totals "based on grade, not ability or gender." Lewark told us, "I never differentiated between boys and girls. My two highest mileage runners ever were both girls." Although most coaches generally keep girls running less than boys, gender differentiation certainly isn't universal.

Steve Kearney promoted gender equality by removing the focus from mileage numbers. He said, "I always believed in equality for the sexes, so we had them run the same *time*, not distance." For example, if a boy runs 350 minutes per week and averages 7:00 pace, that equals 50 miles. If a girl runs 350 minutes per week and averages 8:00 pace, that equals 43.7 miles. While the duration is the same (350 minutes), the girl in this example would run about 87% the number of miles that the boy would run, simply because she is not running at the same pace. The thinking is that on any given run, the body's hard work for a specified number of minutes benefits a girl the same way it benefits a boy, regardless of the number of miles covered. By using time instead of distance, Kearney has eliminated a great deal of guesswork from determining how to differentiate between girls' and boys' mileage.

Karen DeVries, the only female coach in Indiana to win a team championship in cross country, offers experienced insight on girls' mileage. "We typically ran 55-ish miles a week. Not every girl on the team could handle that, but usually the top runners could," she said. While girls' needs may not be exactly the same as boys', DeVries cautions against cutting their mileage and intensity back arbitrarily. "I've only coached girls, and I was never afraid of hard work just because they are girls. I feel like many coaches make the mistake of going easy on their teams just because they are girls. Many girls are tough, and given the chance they will prove it." DeVries saw success in part because she did not view gender as a limitation. She had no qualms about challenging her athletes and pushing them to mileage numbers that exceeded their competition.

Comparing Girls' and Boys' Mileage Data

Throughout my (Derek's) career, I have often heard that the ratio of girls' mileage to boys' should be about ⅔ or ¾. This conventional wisdom puts girls' mileage at about 67-75% the number of boys' mileage. We analyzed the numbers we received from our coaches and found that percentage to be too low. Rick Weinheimer, who has won team state titles in both girls' and boys' cross country, provided the following outline of typical mileage for athletes in his program. When we isolate the Columbus North program, we see that girls run 80-88% of what the boys run.

COLUMBUS NORTH MILEAGE UNDER COACH RICK WEINHEIMER

Grade	Girls	Boys	Percentage
9	35	40	88%
10	42	50	84%
11	49	60	82%
12	56	70	80%

AVERAGE MILEAGE FROM ALL COACHES

Grade	Girls	Boys	Percentage
9	29.5	35.8	82%
10	35.8	44.6	80%
11	42.3	51.7	82%
12	49.3	63.0	78%

We compiled all our coaches' data and identified a statistical mean for each gender and grade. Remember that most of our coaches provided us with ranges of mileage, so for purposes of the following chart we averaged the median of each provided range. Once again, when we compare the girls' mileage to the boys' mileage, we see numbers in the 78-82% range. Some of the most successful girls' coaches in our study consistently required more mileage from their female athletes than conventional wisdom would expect.

Note: The purpose of this chart is to share an average of the data we collected, not to make mileage recommendations for average female and male runners. In answering questions about mileage, coaches typically use their varsity athletes as a standard and adapt from there. Since this chart shows the average of our coaches' responses, it reflects the average mileage of varsity runners, not necessarily the average mileage of all runners on these teams.

Enduring Wisdom

Chapter 14: The Long Run

"The long run is the most important practice of the week."
- Josh Fletcher

Almost all distance runners perform a weekly training ritual known as the long run. One day each week, they intentionally run further than any other day. Since the long run is a staple workout for almost any distance training plan, we asked our coaches to share some thoughts on its role in their training programs.

Its Importance

The long run's importance became clear through the many adjectives the coaches chose to describe it: imperative (Zach Raber), crucial (Colin Altevogt), a staple (Brad Peterson), a pillar (Tim Ray). For Joe Brooks, the importance of the weekly long run increased throughout his career: "During my early coaching days this was not part of my plan. As the seasons went by, this was developed into a 'must do' to be successful."

Chuck Koeppen learned this lesson more fully from coaching his own son. "It was really later in my coaching career when I realized the value of the long run. It was when my son, Charlie, was a junior at Carmel HS. After finishing 32nd in the State XC Meet, he began running 13 miles on his own every Sunday (at a pretty decent pace, I might add). Well, the improvement was immense. He was the Indiana state 3200-meter run champion the following spring in 9:12, winning by six seconds." For Charlie (and for many other athletes) the commitment to a consistent weekly long run led to overall improvement.

Its Length

"Long" means different things to different people, but our coaches quantified their long runs with fairly consistent answers. Most coaches reported long runs in the 8- to 10-mile range, with some as high as 12 miles. Joe Brooks had a simple rule of thumb: "at least an hour." Mark Ellington "generally capped the longest run at 9-10 miles" for the Carmel girls. The longest consistent distance that we observed was a weekly 12-mile long run.

Erhard Bell explained the science behind his approach. "The weekly long run is important, but I believe many programs run *too* long. Research by G. Dudley suggests a saturation response for which exceeding a specific workout duration results in no further increase in aerobic enzyme improvements, and that this time is about 60 minutes" (Dudley, Abraham, & Terjung, 1982). In other words, athletes see diminishing returns after 60 minutes. Many coaches echoed Bell's commentary: a 60 minute weekly long run (or only slightly longer) was very typical.

We've often read in training materials that long runs should make up about 20-25% of a distance runner's total weekly mileage. So we asked our coaches what percentage of weekly volume that 60-minute long run makes up in their programs. From their responses, we established a median percentage range of 17.9-20.4%—just a little lower than the popular 20-25% suggestion. Based on our coaches' median percentages, here is the typical length range for their weekly long runs, based on weekly mileage totals.

Weekly Mileage	Long Run (17.9%)	Long Run (20.4%)
25	4	5
30	5	6
35	6	7
40	7	8
45	8	9
50	9	10
55	10	11
60	11	12

Its Pace

Simply saying that a long run should last 60 minutes does not give a complete picture of the workout. A runner can cover an hour of running in many different ways, so we asked specifically about the intensity level (pace) that the coaches shoot for in their weekly long runs. The majority consensus is that the pace should be fairly easy. Mark Ellington described it as faster than normal recovery run pace, but nowhere near anaerobic threshold pace (more on "anaerobic threshold" in the next chapter). Tim Ray emphasizes "maintaining a comfortable pace, and to limit the number of stops." Coaches seemed more concerned about the uninterrupted duration of the run than about pushing a faster pace.

There is a social component unique to the long run, and coaches embrace its relaxed nature to encourage team bonding and to provide the encouragement of a larger pace group. Mike Prow explained, "The pace is usually easy, especially at the start to keep more kids staying in touch." Eric Kellison, who regularly had athletes running sub-16:00 for 5 kilometers on grass, usually kept long runs at an easy pace, 7:00 per mile (or slightly slower) for high school boys. He described it as "time to kick back and chat it up." Barrie Peterson also appreciated the long run's relationship-building potential. He had his athletes run at "conversational pace, and try to get them to meet up with another runner or runners of equal ability level." Sam Rasmussen's team often ran long after a race at a nearby high school. "They would start to run back to school from the contest and we would either pick them up at a certain mileage point or meet them back at the school...It was part of our culture. Can you imagine what the other teams thought when they saw us show up running from our school or what they thought when we ran home from the meet?" Keep in mind that Rasmussen coached high school cross country 30 years ago, when there were different norms and rules about that sort of thing. He developed his own set of safety guidelines and established routes, accounting for traffic patterns, road surface and width, hills and blind spots, and policies for bad weather. Setting and communicating explicit safety standards allowed his runners more variety and time on the road together.

Which Day of the Week

For most adult runners, Sunday is synonymous with the weekly long run. This holds true for some of our coaches, too, but not as many as we expected. There are rules in Indiana prohibiting high school coaches and athletes from communicating or meeting for practice on Sundays, so most of our coaches (thirteen of them) said that they do their weekly long runs on Mondays instead. Only four of our coaches expect their athletes to do weekly long runs on Sundays without the coach present, creating a culture of high expectations for personal accountability.

Colin Altevogt prefers Mondays, and many others share his rationale: "It makes it a lot easier on them to know we're going to do the long run together at practice." Many coaches like being physically present for the weekly long run and for the athletes to be able to do it together. The social benefits of the long run—both team bonding and improved training motivation—lead them to choose a weekday, when everyone will be there; and Monday allows for the longest recovery time before a Saturday race. Given that they consider it "crucial" and "imperative," it makes sense that most coaches prioritize practice time for the long run.

Variations on the Weekly Long Run

While many of the coaches encouraged a comfortable, conversational pace for their long runs, there were coaches who described some variations to the weekly long run. Karen DeVries did not do a long run weekly; rather, she did it every two weeks. She explained, "I am a believer in long runs and we would typically run ten miles every other week, mainly on Mondays. I have found that it takes two weeks to see the benefits of a longer run." Perhaps one reason DeVries elected to go every other week was the intensity that she required from this workout. Her high school girls would run at "a pretty good clip," which she explained to be as fast as 7:00 pace. Even for a very good high school girl, 10 miles at 7-flat pace is a physically demanding workout.

Josh Fletcher and Brad Peterson both approach long runs as "cut-downs," with athletes starting at a comfortable speed and getting faster throughout the run. Peterson admitted that a long run the day after a race would be at a more comfortable pace, but "when we are rested for the long run then we will run quicker and cut down, get faster as we go. A varsity boy would go from 7:30 down to low-6:00 pace." Fletcher agreed, "We normally do a 'cut down' in our pace each mile. I want their very best effort at the end of the run." Fletcher and Peterson include some anaerobic threshold running late in the long run (again, we'll explain threshold training in the next chapter).

Rick Weinheimer shared another interesting variation on the weekly long run. He believes the long run is "key to teaching the body to recover from glycogen depletion," so he changes his long run with each new phase of the season. In phase one of his cross country training, he bases long runs on total weekly mileage, which is very similar to the other coaches. However, he said, "When we move to phase two intervals, the workout itself becomes a long run with injected faster moments." As his team moves into the racing season, Weinheimer's athletes switch to a continuous interval workout, alternating hard 400 meters with a 600-meter recovery jog. Instead of running an even-paced 10-mile long run, they transition to a workout where they would run 16x400 meters hard with a 600-meter jog recovery in between each one (which is still 10 miles of continuous running).

In our coaches' responses about the weekly long run, we found more similarities than differences. Their comments were very simple. Long runs are not complex, but they are crucial to the long-term development of distance runners. The overall message can be summed up in this statement: If you have the discipline to do your weekly long run correctly and consistently, you will earn the future fruit of your labor.

Enduring Wisdom

Chapter 15: Threshold Training

"Runners who can train longer at their threshold are going to be your top runners."
- Joe Brooks

Threshold training is possibly the most confusing workout for distance coaches to explain. When I (Derek) was a young coach, I asked many different coaches to explain how they design threshold training, and I never got a simple answer. Everyone seems to have a different name for it: anaerobic threshold, lactate threshold, quality sessions, hard sustained run, steady state, tempo run, etc. It also seems that each coach has his or her own definition for what constitutes a threshold workout.

As we received responses to our questions about threshold training, that same complexity emerged. Our coaches' responses were just as complex and varied as their answers about long runs had been simple. Perhaps threshold training is *purposely* complex. Perhaps the variety and ambiguity is an integral part of the design. The fact that coaches struggle to describe it succinctly may actually indicate that they are doing it correctly.

What Is Threshold Pace?

The anaerobic threshold is an exercise intensity range within which the muscles begin accumulating lactic acid and the body is unable to deliver oxygen to the muscles aerobically. Identifying the running pace at which this happens is a little harder. We asked our coaches to define what they consider threshold pace. Their answers varied slightly, so we took a representative sampling of seven coaches' definitions, and we compiled them into the table below.

Barrie Peterson	"30-40 seconds slower per mile than the athlete could race at a 5-mile distance"
Brad Peterson	"30-40 seconds slower than 5k race pace"
Josh Fletcher	"45 seconds to 1 minute slower than an athlete's current 5K pace"
Steve Lewark	"Approximately a minute slower than you can run an all-out mile"
Scott Lidskin	"Roughly 80-90% of 3200 race pace for us"
Sam Rasmussen	"90% of maximum using a heart monitor"
Tim Ray	"About 85% of your race pace"

A number of other coaches described it based on feel rather than with numbers. Many coaches labeled threshold pace "comfortably hard." Sam Rasmussen explained, "Tempo training is where you can barely talk while you're running," and Chuck Koeppen said, "I feel like these runs should run at or near race pace, normally run at a distance less than their standard race distance." Koeppen also talked about doing some longer threshold runs, but for him these threshold runs should simulate the intensity of a race. Most coaches agreed with conventional wisdom that threshold pace is somewhere between 30 and 60 seconds per mile slower than 5K race pace. Two coaches—Rick Weinheimer and Colin Altevogt—were slower to give definite parameters to the pace of threshold workouts, not wanting to define it as a single pace.

Altevogt was Weinheimer's assistant for three years, and both coaches hold a similar mentality toward threshold training. Both follow "Paavo" training, the method named for Finnish runner Paavo Nurmi, adapting Paavo's focus on even pacing to their own programs. Weinheimer alternates between a short threshold run and a long threshold run. He does not label these runs specifically as threshold workouts, but with his permission that is what we will call them. Weinheimer explains that his athletes run these workouts essentially "all out." If they are running a 4 mile SPPM (short pace per mile) workout, the goal is to run 4 miles as hard as they can. If an athlete is running an 8 mile LPPM (long pace per mile) workout, the goal is to run 8 miles as hard as they can. Here's how Weinheimer explains the relationship between the SPPM and the LPPM: "With an eye toward maximizing the Long PPM in terms of distance and pace, the SPPM helps improve the second aspect: pace. By forcing the body to push a faster pace for a shorter distance (SPPM), physically the body must tolerate an earlier and more abrupt bout of oxygen debt. When the body adapts to this and to the more rapid leg turnover, on the LPPM runners are physically (and mentally) more prepared for a slighter slower pace and slightly slower dip into heavy breathing, which allows them to run farther and faster than they would without the SPPM." Weinheimer's SPPM and LPPM work together to push the aerobic threshold ever higher.

Altevogt adds, "I think the key for us is not providing a range of target times. I feel that telling [the athletes] to run 'the best they can' (essentially 'all out' but we never say those words to make it a little less intimidating) is a lot more effective than providing them some ambiguous time range." For Altevogt, giving the athletes subjective instructions for running the best they can on that day (instead of specific pace ranges) produces more effective threshold workouts.

(For more information about Paavo training, see my IndianaRunner.com article in Appendix B.)

Intentional Variations

The strongest pattern that emerged from the coaches' comments was the intentional variety they give to threshold training. While long runs are very similar from week to week, threshold workouts change dramatically throughout the course of a season. This could explain why so many coaches struggle to explain succinctly this aspect of training: threshold workouts in June can look very different from threshold workouts in October.

Chuck Koeppen said of threshold training, "You always want to mix it up. Variety is the spice of life." Erhard Bell used the same expression: "I also believe variety is crucial to avoid mental boredom with the quality sessions (something I have changed from years in the past). Variety is the spice of life!" Koeppen and Bell coached together at Carmel for four years, so it is unsurprising that they shared this phraseology. Yet the sentiment wasn't particular to Carmel: threshold variety was prevalent throughout all of the coaches' responses.

One way that coaches create variety is in the running surface. Josh Fletcher changes locations for threshold workouts. "We do tempo runs on a rotation of grass, wooded trails, and roads." Mark Ellington often sought out rolling hills and softer surfaces as the season progressed. "We try to move these [runs] to grassy locations and frequently try to get on the course at Northview [Christian Church] because of the hillier terrain," he said.

Zach Raber varies the intensity based on the distance. "When we do tempo runs, we typically shoot for 86-90% of VO2 max. Dr. Jack Daniels has a great chart, so does Greg McMillan. If we are doing a short tempo effort, say 3 miles, we will do it more at the 90% speed. If we are doing a longer tempo of 5-7 miles, we will focus on staying at 86-88%" (Daniels, 1998/2005). (By "VO2 max," Raber means the intensity level at which the body delivers its maximum volume of oxygen to the muscles. We'll discuss VO2 max more in the next chapter on interval training.) Raber varies the length and intensity of his tempo runs, but his workouts always fit within the basic parameters of a threshold workout (McMillan, 2016).

We asked Scott Lidskin for a sample threshold workout for a high school girl who he would expect to run 19:00 for cross country (5K on grass). True to the complex nature of threshold training, he gave examples in three varieties: "We would probably do three different 'long' threshold workouts with her in cross country: 1) A 5k continuous threshold run on the track at 6:30-45 pace. 2) A four-mile continuous threshold run on the grass at 6:45-6:55 pace. 3) 2x2 miles on the track or grass at 6:30-40 pace (with 3 minutes' rest)." Here is yet another example of a coach varying pace, distance, and running surface in order to mix up threshold training.

Eric Kellison's athletes would progress through a variety of threshold workouts over the summer. "I want my best guys to be able to run 5-6 miles at 6:00 pace by the first day of [summer] practice. We run this pace along with 2 x 2 miles x 2 sets throughout the summer. We would vary distance, rest, and tempo as the summer progressed." There you see it again: the intentional variation to threshold training, manipulating different aspects of the workout to constantly mix it up. None of our coaches named a single threshold workout that they do repeatedly.

Instead, they regularly mix up threshold workouts with intentional variations.

Length of a Threshold Run

We asked coaches to quantify the length of a threshold run, and the table below shows their answers. Some coaches measured in minutes while some tracked miles covered. Conventional wisdom says that 20 minutes is a gold standard for an anaerobic threshold workout. Interestingly, every coach who answered in minutes used 20 minutes as the bottom end of threshold training, except Steve Lewark, who breaks longer tempos into 20-minute segments (You'll read more about Lewark's approach below). Most of our coaches challenge their athletes to push more into the 30- to 40-minute range for threshold runs.

Coach	Minutes	Mileage
Barrie Peterson	20 - 35	
Brad Peterson	20 - 35	
Colin Altevogt	20 - 45	3 – 8
Erhard Bell		2 – 7
Eric Kellison		3 – 8
Josh Fletcher		4 – 8
Karen DeVries		3 – 4
Mike Prow	20 - 40	
Steve Lewark	12 – 20 (segments)	
Zach Raber		3 – 7
Tim Ray	30	

Threshold Running All Season

We have mentioned periodization, or the breaking up of a season into a series of phases. Almost every cross country coach we know uses this idea of training phases in some way, often moving from "base" mileage in the summer to intervals and speed work in the fall. Barrie Peterson trains in phases too, but he was careful to explain the variety he keeps within each phase: "My coaching philosophy might be a bit unique, but I try to have all phases of training in all parts of the season; i.e., long runs, tempo runs, repetition and interval training, speed work, etc." While he does emphasize a certain type of workout during its specified phase, he thinks it is essential to keep every physiological system working throughout the season. He doesn't wait until the "threshold phase" to include some threshold pace running in his plan, and he keeps threshold workouts going even when some coaches have moved on to shorter, faster intervals. It turns out that, among the elite coaches, Peterson's philosophy is not uncommon at all. While coaches definitely periodize, they maintain variety, keeping threshold training a part of their weekly regimen throughout the season. Eric Kellison explained, "We do hard workouts year round. I feel this keeps the runners motivated, and it is a good way to stay in shape." For most of our coaches, threshold training plays a part in every phase of their training, right on up to the state meet. (For a great explanation of this kind of training, check out *Take the Lead* by Scott Simmons and Will Freeman [2006]. They recommend a "diamond approach" that builds up all training components during every phase of the season.)

Tim Ray includes in his summer base phase some fartlek runs (continuous running while alternating fast and slow), and then he usually starts sustained threshold workouts after 6 weeks of base running, as soon as his athletes have built up some general aerobic fitness. Erhard Bell said, "While we maintain these longer intervals and tempo runs during the season, we begin to incorporate shorter intervals as the season progresses."

None of our coaches talked about threshold workouts being exclusively a preseason workout. They may begin adding shorter, faster workouts, but they never abandon threshold runs. Instead, they strategically tweak threshold training throughout the season, going from gentler fartlek runs, to sustained tempos, to long intervals at threshold pace.

Maximizing Time at Threshold Pace

For Sam Rasmussen, the pace was the whole point of threshold training. Rasmussen explained, "Instead of being concerned with the distance, we are concerned with the time over that distance. The key to tempo training lies in the speed of the run, maintaining a consistent and specific pace." Like Rasmussen, most of our coaches were less concerned with the length of the threshold run than with maintaining the proper pace. Because of this concern, several coaches end up splitting the threshold run into a number of shorter segments, allowing the athlete to accumulate more time at threshold pace.

When we looked previously at the length of a threshold run, Steve Lewark was an outlier, with a 20-minute run being the high end of his range. He explained, "The longest we would run [continuously] at tempo is 20 minutes, and that would be only for the experienced runners. Most of the others would be between 12 and 18 minutes. I don't believe high school athletes can really maintain the tempo pace I want them to for longer than that." That is, unless they get a short rest. Lewark breaks up most workouts into shorter runs with very short recovery periods in between. "Most runners can handle at least 50% more minutes by breaking it up...experienced runners can handle 40 minutes at tempo pace when broken up, even with a very short recovery—about a minute for most distances." For this to work, coaches must keep the recovery time really short. Most coaches who split their threshold runs said 2 minutes of rest is the maximum in between bouts.

Tim Ray does 1000-meter tempo intervals with only one minute of recovery time. Steve Kearney's intervals are similar: "We did repeat Ks on a very fast loop, trying to match the slowest K of each kid's race, no faster. Five, building to eight [by the end of the season]. We had four or five groups to allow for short rest of no more than 90 seconds." Scott Lidskin shared a workout where athletes would run "5 x 800 @ 85-90% of 3200 race pace with 1 minute of rest."
Mark Ellington shared how his split-tempos progressed throughout the season. "Initially these threshold/tempo workouts are in sets of minutes. Examples would include: 2 x 12 minutes or 2 x 10 minutes for our top athletes, 2 x 7-8 minutes for our JV groups. As we progress, the time structure changes over to 3 x mile, 2 x 2 mile, and even 3 x 8-10 minutes."

One way coaches commonly break up threshold training is to split the tempo run into 2-mile segments. Zach Raber said, "occasionally we will do split tempo runs of 2-3 x 2 miles with 2 minutes of rest." Brad Peterson added, "I also really like 2-3 x 1.5 mile repeats for girls and 2x2 miles for boys (on occasion, for a stud, 3x2 miles)." As long as the rest time was very short, these coaches found the additional distance at threshold pace to be beneficial. Brad Peterson also mentioned another benefit of running a split tempo:

"Now they are running much closer to race pace for these, perhaps within 15 or 20 seconds per mile."

Correlating Threshold Running to Racing

We observed a number of coaches who, like Peterson above, made direct connections between threshold workouts and races. Joe Brooks even said, "Racing is a form of threshold training, so I took that into consideration in my training plan." Our coaches saw threshold workouts as physical and mental preparation for a grueling 5K cross country race. Karen DeVries explained, "[Threshold running] teaches the girls to keep their heads up and be ready for a move that they have but a moment to respond to. This is mimicking the race and, like I said earlier, everything we do is to prepare for the state meet."

Think about a 5K race. Most high school runners start out fast in the first mile, find themselves in oxygen debt in the middle of the race, and still have a lot of ground to cover before the finish line. Mike Prow and his assistant coach Aaron Crague devised an interesting way to use threshold training as race preparation. Prow explained, "At the end of my career with Aaron Crague, we were doing tempo miles on the track, 5:20-5:40, as a kind of warmup before we got to the 'meat and potatoes' of the *real* workout." By starting a track workout with a hard tempo mile, Prow and Crague were simulating the athletes' race experience and teaching their bodies to deal with the oxygen debt they would encounter mid-race.

While many coaches maintain that tempo pace should be distinct from all-out effort, others intentionally don't hold back during threshold runs. Colin Altevogt challenges conventional threshold training wisdom. "'Comfortably hard' is a popular phrase in regards to threshold/tempo running, but the essence of a distance race is maximizing discomfort to achieve optimal results, so what are we teaching our athletes by forcing them to stay comfortable?" Without race-day adrenaline and competition, most runners do not quite achieve race pace over an equivalent distance in practice, even with an all-out effort. So the threshold pace stays distinct from "race pace," without compromising his runners' preparation for hard racing. In Altevogt's mind, threshold training should prepare athletes for the reality of the race, mentally as well as physically.

Enduring Wisdom

Chapter 16: Interval Training

"Bread and butter ... Kilometers late season."
- Eric Kellison

When you think of interval training, there's a good chance you think of "K repeats," a kilometer-length interval workout that is commonly part of 5K training. Our coaches also talked of these 1000-meter repeats, but their approach to interval training wasn't quite that simple. We found that coaches use interval training in different ways throughout the cross country season, sometimes even before any designated "interval phase" of the season begins. Barrie Peterson told us, "I *never* get too far away from some kind of repetition and/or interval training; we simply up the ante (numbers-wise and distance-wise) as the season progresses." Joe Brooks agreed that interval training can be adapted throughout the season: "There are all kinds of workouts you can do with intervals that can get desired benefits." The coaches shared many ways to use interval workouts, depending on their goals. This chapter explains their thoughts on interval training, with some of their sample interval workouts at the end.

But first, a definition. At its simplest, interval training can be understood as a series of relatively short, repeated hard runs with rest in between. But for many coaches who include a specific interval phase to their training, it is helpful to distinguish between interval pace and threshold pace, especially since so many coaches experiment with split tempos at threshold pace. So what's the difference? Erhard Bell explained, "To me interval (speed) training is faster than lactate-threshold velocity but not quicker than 800-meter race pace." Bell makes a clear distinction between a faster-paced interval workout (commonly called VO2 interval training*), and the anaerobic threshold training we discussed in the last chapter.

An athlete's "VO2 max" measures the maximum volume of oxygen that an athlete can use while running. See Daniels Running Formula (1998/2005) for a more complete explanation of VO2 Interval training.

When to Start Intervals

An interval-focused training phase usually begins after athletes have done plenty of base mileage (phase 1) and threshold training (a typical phase 2 emphasis). For most teams, interval training becomes the third, most intense phase, coinciding with the fall racing season. Indiana's early season racing usually begins in late August or early September, at which time coaches usually begin interval training.

A number of coaches told us they start in August. Joe Brooks started interval training "the first week of practice" (usually the first week of August in Indiana). Josh Fletcher normally started interval workouts in "middle to late August." Brad Peterson started long intervals "typically in late August with most experienced runners." Steve Lewark said, "We start immediately doing intervals at tempo pace and adding a few faster intervals the last half of the season." Other coaches elected to wait a little longer. Sam Rasmussen's interval training "usually came in September." Chuck Koeppen said, "We would start our Interval training usually mid to late September." Mark Ellington waited as well. "We don't start our interval work until the end of September after our regular season has ended," he said.

Some coaches implement intervals, perhaps shorter and perhaps at threshold pace, throughout the summer training, but most don't begin a VO2 interval training phase until late August or early September, approximately 6-10 weeks before the Indiana state meet.

Approach Intervals Cautiously

It is with good reason that coaches wait so long to begin VO2 interval training. When it comes to training for a 5K, interval training is the most intense running that an athlete will do. Conventional wisdom says that overuse injuries are the result of running too many miles, and weekly training volume is clearly a factor in running injuries. However, an emerging school of thought says running injuries could be primarily a factor of implementing interval (speed) training too early or too vigorously. And besides the physical intensity, these workouts require great mental and emotional energy, which would be hard to maintain all the way from June through October.

Scott Lidskin explained, "Interval workouts are called VO2 workouts for us, and we approach them very carefully. We believe that competitive high school athletes can have the tendency to 'race' a bit too much in practice, and that can be dangerous (though it can be good in some instances too)." Tim Ray agreed: "We are very careful with interval training. We have experienced in previous seasons that we have overdone it in this phase, and it has cost us. Make sure the volume of intervals coincides with the rest of the program. Don't do too much, thinking that there are huge dividends at the end of the rainbow. Usually, this spells disaster. Always err on too few rather than too many." Lidskin and Ray both implement hard interval workouts with their athletes; they do not neglect the clear benefits of interval training. Instead, they take a thoughtful, cautious approach.

Transition with Fartleks

Fartlek training serves as a gentle transition from base training to interval training for three of our coaches. *Fartlek*, which means "speed play" in Swedish, means continuous running during which some segments are faster and other segments are slower. Fartleks can be an important part of the cautious approach that Lidskin and Ray discussed above. Coaches can design endless combinations of fartlek workouts, manipulating every aspect of the run to increase intensity gradually in preparation for the interval phase.

Zach Raber didn't want to start interval training too abruptly. "During our summer training, our athletes do fartlek runs of up to 25 minutes of hard running [not counting the easy segments]. This gives them a great base for being able to do quality interval sessions when the season begins." He wanted his athletes' bodies to be prepared for the intensity that interval training requires. Similarly, Mike Prow uses fartlek runs when he wants his athletes to adapt to shorter recovery time. "In August and September I like to have a little less recovery than the run itself, so we can do fartlek running to vary the rest interval time." Longer hard segments and shorter recovery periods in late summer helped Prow's athletes transition to the demanding interval workouts of the fall.

Sam Rasmussen appreciated the carefree feel of summer fartlek training as a less-intense way to prepare his athletes for the interval training that was to come. "Summer was a fun time to try and run all of the fartlek training we could through woods, farm fields and parks around our area. We always thought that fartlek training was unstructured and fun. Everyone seemed to enjoy the running and worked hard at it. We never stopped running; we just varied the distance and speeds."

From Long to Short

Once a team is physically ready for the intense interval phase, they begin with length. Most of our coaches affirmed the importance of moving from longer intervals in August or September to shorter ones as the tournament time approaches. Sam Rasmussen, after preparing with all those summer fartleks, espoused "longer distance intervals in the beginning of the training and shorter ones as the season progresses." As interval length decreases, the pace often increases and gets closer to goal race pace. Below are some examples of how coaches implement longer intervals early and shorten them down as the season develops.

Karen DeVries:
"We usually start with two-mile repeats, and because of the time of year this serves three purposes. It continues to build a base, builds strength, and gets the team used to running hard together. September/October intervals would consist of mile repeats, 1200 repeats, that introduce a quicker leg turnover."

Joe Brooks:
"We did 4-5 mile repeats (2-3 minutes' rest) in August and 6-8 1000-meter repeats (2 minutes' rest) in September. In October, 16 rhythm 400s would be 70-75 [seconds] with about 30 seconds' rest."

Colin Altevogt:
"In the latter stages of our base phase (like August), we occasionally might do repeat miles or repeat 2Ks. This

helps us to transition to hard running on the grass since our threshold runs are always done on a paved trail."

Steve Kearney:
"Our threshold intervals were about all we did until October. Then we added a day of 8x200 to 8x400 with a fairly long recovery jog."

Brad Peterson:
"August: mile repeats at current date [race] pace with 2 minutes rest. September: more of what we already did. Also 16-20 x 400 with 45-60 seconds rest, starting at goal race pace and getting slightly faster as it goes. 800 repeats are also good in mid September at 5K goal pace with 2 minutes rest."

Recovery Within the Workout

The length of each bout of running, the overall volume of the workout, and the intensity of the pace are important components of an interval workout. But do not forget to plan for another important factor: what the athlete will do between the hard bouts of running, and for how long.

Almost all our coaches keep the recovery time equal to or less than the time spent running. Karen DeVries explained, "If they run hard for six minutes, they get a six-minute rest. If they run hard for twelve minutes, they get a nine-minute rest. Yet, it all depends on what we are trying to accomplish. Sometimes the rest time is less." Josh Fletcher said, "I like hills, 1000s, mile and 2000-meter repeats, normally with 1 to 1 rest." Chuck Koeppen said, "Recovery time was usually somewhat near the time of the actual interval that was run." Because a 5K cross country race is so oxygen-dependent, it makes sense to minimize rest time during an interval workout to more accurately simulate the race.

Another way to replicate the demands of the race is to implement active recovery, during which the athlete is always running, always keeping the heart rate and breathing levels elevated. Mike Prow remembered his college training, saying, "A great interval workout we did at Butler University and [later at] Valparaiso HS was up to 20 times a 400 with a 200-meter [jog recovery]. I believe in interval or repetition running that you stay actively jogging during the majority of your recovery time." Rick Weinheimer agrees. His athletes are never standing still during a cross country workout. Weinheimer explained, "Our interval work in cross country is entirely done with jog rest intervals to maximize oxygen delivery benefit." Sam Rasmussen echoed the same idea: "We did spurts of intervals during the run but never stopped running after the interval. We certainly brought the pace down in order to recover for the next interval."

The way that a coach structures the recovery portion of an interval workout is really important. You could design a 5x1000-meter repeat workout with 10 minutes' standing rest between each bout, but that does not replicate the demands of a 5K cross country race. By minimizing recovery time or using active jog recovery (or both), the coaches may be slowing down the intensity of the hard bouts, but they are more properly preparing the athletes for the race.

Sample Interval Workouts

Below are some additional examples of specific interval workouts that our coaches do or did with their teams.

Scott Lidskin:
"A typical VO2 workout for us would be 4-5 x 1000 at 3200 race pace with 3:30 rest."

Mike Prow:
"6x1000 @ 3:00 with 3:00 jog recovery or 3 x 1 mile around 5 minutes with 5 minutes' recovery."

Erhard Bell:
"Intervals include: (1) 10K pace intervals: 2000-meter intervals, 3-4 total with recovery 25% of the interval, (2) 5K pace intervals: 1200-meter intervals, 3-5 total with recovery 75% of interval."

Zach Raber:
"Examples: boy in 16:00 shape. girl in 19:30 shape.
August: 5-7x1000, boy- 3:05-3:10 with 2:00-2:30 rest, girl- 3:45-3:51 with 2-3 minutes' rest.
Late September: boy- 4-5 x 1 mile @ 4:52 with equal rest, girls- 3-4 x 1 mile @ 5:55 with equal rest."

Mark Ellington:
"6 x 1k repeats. Athletes [girls] hit between 3:30 and 3:40 per kilometer and have 3 minutes to recover."

Colin Altevogt:
"When we've switched to intervals, we do 400s at a prescribed time. The time stays the same all season, but the workout is made harder by jogging the rest at a faster pace and/or taking less rest time between intervals. By requiring them to jog in between, it makes the cumulative effect of all the intervals very taxing."

Josh Fletcher:
"One of my favorite workouts in September is 3 x 2000 with 5-6 minutes of walking rest. I look to athletes to get faster on each interval and faster from the first to second 1000 in each interval."

Chuck Koeppen:
"An example would be 6x1000 @ 3:10 on 6-minute 'goes' (this would be for guys). The pace was for the most part race-pace." [Six-minute "goes" means

everyone begins the next set every six minutes. Therefore recovery time differs for each athlete based on how soon they finish.]

Eric Kellison:
"Summer: 2 x 2 miles x 2 sets at 13 minutes with 10 minutes' rest between intervals.
In season: Tuesday—5 x 1 mile on grass at 5:30-6:00 pace on 10-minute 'goes.'
Thursday—5 x 1K on hilly grass loop at 3:30-3:45 on 6-minute 'goes.'"

Tim Ray:
"We try and do these on a relatively flat surface that is soft. An example workout that we have done is 8x1000 meters with 3:00 rest."

Steve Lewark:
"During the second half of the season we would include other paces with our tempo intervals. An example of this is a 3200 at tempo, an 800 at 20 seconds faster per mile than tempo, 2x400 at 40 seconds per mile faster than tempo, and finishing with another 3200 at tempo."

Rick Weinheimer:
"10x400 at goal pace with a 3:30 jog between each one, and with a double jog after every set of four."

Karen Devries:
"We have an excellent 1200 interval that is tough and mimics areas of the state course."

Zach Raber:
"We'll typically start with 800s, then move to 1000s, then up to mile repeats, then back down to 1000s as we get into the tournament season."

Barrie Peterson:

"Bobby Moldovan did this during his senior year of cross country: Early season—3 x mile at 5:20 with 4 minutes' rest, 8 x 1/2 mile at 2:38 with 2-3 minutes' rest, 12 x 400 at 68 with 90 seconds' rest. Mid- to late-season—5 x mile at 5:10 with 3-4 minutes' rest, 10 x ½ mile at 2:31 with 2 minutes' rest, 20 x 400 at 71 with 60 seconds' rest."

Chapter 17: Training Lessons Learned

"There is no one training program that is correct.
That is the most important thing that I've learned."
- Scott Lidskin

Learning proper training for distance runners takes study, but it also takes experience with trial and error. We asked the coaches what they'd learned about training, and in this chapter we will share their answers. For this particular topic, we will simply to provide each response verbatim. **Question Posed:** "What is the single most important lesson that you learned about training that helped you in your development of coaching high school cross country? When and how did you learn that lesson?"

Colin Altevogt

The most important thing is base and building strength. In 2009 when I was an assistant coach at Columbus North, we went from starting intervals very early in previous years and doing a lot more typical "workouts" (fast intervals with standing rest) to doing much more strength-based workouts by holding onto our base longer and doing intervals with jogging rest almost exclusively. Those were pretty good teams and continued to be good for the next few years after that.

Erhard Bell

The single most important item I have learned regarding coaching runners is *never* to forget the basics of recovery. These include (1) Proper nutrition including monitoring for iron-deficiency anemia with CBC [complete blood count] and serum ferritin before each season, (2) Re-hydration, (3) Adequate sleep, (4) Injury prevention, (5) Illness prevention, and (6) Monitoring morning pulse and weight to determine response to training. I attempt to develop my training sessions by using the latest scientific developments in running science, which means you have to change things from time to time! I use my Southport [High School, where Bell was a student-athlete] distance training program as a guide with a goal of developing consistent training, use pacing charts for each individual runner, keep track of training in a daily training log, and utilize proper training progression to develop fitness and avoid injury. I also incorporate general strength training, utilize supplemental training and add sufficient mental preparation to complete the program. I initially utilized the Jack Daniels training program, moved to the Rick Weinheimer program and then updated it to my current training. My current approach I believe can develop the best fitness and running skills while avoiding the multiple injuries that result from overtraining.

Joe Brooks

An important lesson I learned about training high school boys was that they have to buy into what you are selling. They need to know why they are training this way. Daily conversations need to take place. Every day we had a team meeting to establish this dialogue. They need to see results of previous runners and previous teams who have done this training as well as results for themselves. In our locker room, we had the "Top 10" runner board for each class hung from the ceiling. We had all the years of Warren Central teams that won a Sectional, Regional, Semi-State or State title. Tradition is very powerful. Goals need to be established and rewards need to be in place when runners achieve their goals, whether it is an individual goal or a team goal. I learned this lesson from Dick Conway the very first year I was his assistant coach at Warren Central in 1980.

Karen DeVries

Training is a process and consistency is a key. I learned that in high school because I was on a very successful team, and for four years I saw how the cumulative training only helped me improve each year, and even stay free from injury. It is also about doing many things right, not just one thing. Anyone can have a good day, but if a lot of things aren't being done right, then there might not be so many "good" days. I believe just training cannot be the single goal to achieve success, because so many factors are involved. Ultimately though, everything that happens is planned by God for our good and His glory. God has blessed myself and my teams, and He has also put obstacles in my path to teach me for His purpose and my good. Every blessing I have received has come from God, and I was just a vessel He used.

Mark Ellington

Strength training is key. There is so much information out there, and there are many knowledgeable individuals that can be tapped; take advantage of that. It's never been an area of strength for me as a coach. I've learned quite a bit, but I still am not the lead on our coaching staff. St. Vincent's Sports Performance has been a tremendous partner for us. Not only have they helped the coaching staff, they have worked directly with our athletes to develop better dynamic warm-up routines and provided instruction on proper form in strength drills. In the first 2-3 seasons I coached, we dealt with major injuries with a few athletes. Matt and Kelly Wire (assistant coaches) researched strategies that might help address these injury concerns. A strength routine was developed and SVSP was also a part of that development. Since that time there have been tweaks and adjustments, but I believe that has made a big difference in our level of sustained success.

Josh Fletcher

Be patient. To me being patient is remembering how long the season is to a high school athlete. It is important to "peak" at the right time. I think too many coaches get too excited early in the season, and by the end the athletes are too tired (mentally and physically) to perform at their best. In 2000, I had a really good boys' cross country team, 10 guys sub-17:00 for 5k. By the time we got to the state finals, they were mentally and physically exhausted and finished in 18th place. When I looked back on our training, I noticed we did too much too early in August and September. The following year we only lost one kid and we finished 5th with basically the same group with more patiently designed and placed workouts.

Steve Kearney

Learning that you always have to hold the high achievers back so they don't bash themselves into the ground. I once learned that when I let a top athlete run 4-5 miles Sundays on her own. She was running on fumes for a few Saturdays in a row. She admitted that the 4-5 miles consisted of 12x300 uphill with a jog back!

Eric Kellison

In cross country kids need to train hard, but not all out. My guys never really were asked to train all out in the cross country season. Endurance is more important than flat-out speed. I learned this my second or third year of coaching after reading several books and talking to coaches.

Chuck Koeppen

Just trying not to be too overzealous. I learned this after 3-4 years of coaching at Carmel. I love the sport, I love coaching....and I would get this group of guys and gals in late summer, and I just could not hold back! Sometimes I know that we did too much. But in coaching you are always learning....and believe me, I learned. Don't do too much too early! Also, I can attest to the fact that "Champions are made during the off-season!" I believe that is absolutely fact...100% of the time!

Steve Lewark

Training at tempo pace. When I was in high school and college, the training staple was repeat 400's at a pretty fast pace almost daily. During my first years coaching, I did a lot more interval workouts at a faster pace than tempo pace. We were fairly successful doing this, as I had two girls' teams place 5th and an individual state champion. However, through experimentation and listening to speakers at the track clinics, such as Dr. Chapman, I transitioned to doing most of the interval training at tempo pace and reducing one interval session per week.

Scott Lidskin

There is no one training program that is correct. That is the most important thing that I've learned. Certainly, there is a huge amount of science involved in creating a training schedule. However, there are some teams that need to be trained with the idea of improving their mental toughness, so we might push the envelope of correct science. Other teams might be physically young or fragile, and we'll "under train" compared to what we think that they can physiologically handle. I learned this in 2000 when we tried to train like our 1998 state championship team and our top-10 1999 team and we completely broke down physically (our coaching staff refers to that 2000 season as our Voldemort season).

Barrie Peterson

As mentioned in my answer to a previous question, the single most important lesson that I learned about training a high school runner (or any other runner, for that matter) is that every athlete is different in how they respond to quantity and quality of training. Therefore, it is extremely important to individualize workouts as much as humanly possible. For instance, Johnny might thrive on huge amounts of interval training and maximum mileage, while Jimmy cannot handle that kind of mileage and intensity of training. Johnny might be doing 20-24 x 400 intervals, but Jimmy will get just as much out of 16-18 x 400; and Johnny might do a 12 mile long run, while Jimmy will only do 6-8 miles. There is a "point of no return" for every athlete. As a coach, you need to determine what that "point" is for all of your athletes. The longer that you have a particular athlete (freshman to senior), the more you will learn about this aspect of training through trial and error. The importance of going *easy* on *easy* days also cannot be stressed enough. And at certain times in the season, either as a team or individually, the principle of "less is more" should not be ignored. I have always been a kind of "seat of your pants" kind of coach; and this has paid off—you must stay flexible in your thinking and workout preparation!

Brad Peterson

Individualization. Every single runner is different. Brett Tipton would have been horrible with a long run every Sunday. He would have hated it and it would have taken away his freshness in his legs. He liked having that pop. Middle distance runners need that pop. That's when I learned that, through Brett.

Longer distance runners typically thrive on more mileage and feel better with that. Giving every single kid some love and knowing their personal bests and improvements in workouts and in races. Showing them all that you care about them as runners and as people.

Mike Prow

Rest is important. I learned that from Jason Casiano who started running at The University of Wisconsin in 1991 and said he would get 2 days of easy recovery runs following a race.

Zach Raber

The greatest lesson I learned was consistency. If you can have consecutive year long cycles of injury free running and steady increases in mileage, you will have success as a coach and athlete. Dr. Jack Daniels and Dr. Joe Vigil talk about this a lot. Both of those coaches have obviously had a tremendous amount of success.

Sam Rasmussen

Listen to your runners and respond to how they feel. Encourage them to ask questions about the training and be sure to answer their questions to their satisfaction. Remember that there is no race more important than the health and welfare of the student-athlete under your charge. There is no training workout that has to be accomplished at the sacrifice of your runner's health and welfare.

Tim Ray

First year of coaching, we had 15 student-athletes on our team. Of those 15, three of them were dealing with stress fractures. I learned very early that more is not better. Every runner needs to be treated differently within the framework of the program. I also learned that each season is different. Go into a season with a plan, but don't be afraid to change or adjust the plan. Also, try new things that you think might work. If they do, great. If the results are not what you thought they were going to be, don't panic. This is how you learn what works and what doesn't. There are really, really smart coaches out there. Talk and absorb as much information as possible from all coaches.

Rick Weinheimer

That cross country is ALL about oxygen. If two runners are equal in talent, leg speed, and toughness, the one with the most oxygen capacity will always win. In 2009 I made the commitment to devote all our cross country training to oxygen development and to remove all anaerobic training during that season. Runners still get the little anaerobic work they need for cross country by racing, and they now have all those days previously devoted to anaerobic to be oxygen delivery workouts. I had been thinking about our phase-1 training, which is entirely aerobic, and thinking about teams that would race better even if they only did our phase 1. At that moment I realized what we should do (saving our last phase of anaerobic training for track season). I discussed it with our senior team captains, who embraced the idea.

Conclusion: A Shared Future

"We tried to make everyone feel like part of the family. I think this made everyone try to run their best."
- Steve Lewark

Looking Ahead

We have written this book because so many of these legendary coaches have left the profession. In fact, since we started this project, two more of them announced their retirement (Mark Ellington and Rick Weinheimer). As we send this book to be published, only four of the 19 coaches that we interviewed remain active high school cross country coaches in Indiana.

Many of the coaches in this book are "baby boomers" (the generation born between 1946 and 1964), and they leave a void of knowledge and experience, what authors Dorothy Leonard and Walter Swap call "deep smarts" (Leonard & Swap, 2005). "Deep smarts" refers to the know-how that comes with years of experience and doesn't translate well to guidebooks and training manuals. Deep smarts are easily lost when leaders retire. The challenge for the next generation of coaches will be to engage fresh thinking about new challenges without disregarding the solid foundation these older coaches have built.

Colin Altevogt is the only coach in this study from the millennial generation (born between 1981 and 1997). Will other young coaches emerge to lead powerhouse programs to state championships? Will they stick around at the same high school for 30 years like so many of their predecessors did? We cannot answer these questions, but we can give new coaches a bit of history on which to build.

This book is our attempt to start a conversation between two generations of coaches, to keep our sport thriving. It is only a place to start. We couldn't possibly capture all the coaches' "deep smarts" in a book. But we hope to inspire new coaches to mine their own professional networks and learn from the coaches that came before them.

What Great Coaches Have in Common

In all our coaches' stories and advice, one main theme emerged: the value of positively engaging with people. A coach at any age can benefit from emulating these coaches' interactions with those around them. Despite many personal differences, their approach was strikingly similar: They seek to listen and learn, they are organized but flexible, and they are inclusive servant-leaders.

Great Coaches Learn and Listen

Coaches everywhere expect their athletes to work hard toward improvement, and the coaches in this book practice what they preach. Despite being some of the most successful coaches in our sport's history, they continually seek out new ideas and ways to improve. Like most of these coaches, Barrie Peterson began coaching without any formal training; his career has been a combination of intentional study with his self-described "seat-of-the-pants learning," and 50 years later he is still open to new ideas. That kind of tenacious pursuit of improvement characterizes all 19 of the coaches we spoke with: growth, rather than accolades, is often their primary goal. Not that these coaches don't care about winning; they are very competitive, and they expect excellence from their teams. But what struck us was that even more than demanding excellence from their athletes, they set an example by demanding excellence from themselves. As

Tim Ray put it, great coaches "want the best out of their athletes and expect the same from themselves." Rick Weinheimer considers continuous learning vital to his coaching success, and Karen DeVries pointed out that great satisfaction accompanies success only when that success comes through hard work. Sam Rasmussen captured the ethos of all 19 when he told us, "I never stopped looking for answers on how to be better."

In the everyday of coaching, that hard work can look different than you might expect: it looks like listening. These are true experts in their field, with plenty of knowledge to share. Yet when asked what makes a great coach, almost all of them considered it important to be a listener. Eric Kellison's strength as a listener helps him to communicate well and "get everyone on the same page." One of Brad Peterson's strengths is another kind of "listening": being very observant of his athletes. Listening is a generous act: it gives athletes a sense of significance and empowers them to live up to high expectations. It is an act of respect. In Rick Stover's words, "Earned respect and trust are vital not only from athlete to coach, but coach to athlete."

Great Coaches Are Organized but Flexible

Almost every coach said being organized is essential to success. "Detail oriented" and "organized" showed up over and over again in our survey responses about the most important characteristics of a great coach. Even those who aren't naturally organized in other parts of life have made it a priority in their coaching career. "I take a lot of time to organize my practice plans and race plans," said Zach Raber. Even those who didn't use the word "organized" spent time making and communicating a clear plan for each season, often rooted in their studies of physiology and the science of training. Eric Kellison emphasized long- and short-term planning and documenting workouts and races.

The art of coaching comes in applying those plans and data to meet the needs of individual athletes: in other words, being flexible. Erhard Bell compared coaching to practicing medicine. He finds that in both fields the science must be combined efficiently with the very personal art of understanding people's needs—an idea that echoes Steve Kearney's approach of beginning with the science of training and finishing with flexibility and creativity. Colin Altevogt brought up the need to adjust to unforeseen circumstances, and Josh Fletcher emphasized seeing the big picture and being patient to implement the long-term plan. The dual priorities of structure and flexibility lead to success.

Great Coaches are Inclusive Servant-Leaders

Noticeably absent from our coaches' comments was the idea of maintaining control. We saw zero references to demanding respect and compliance. Instead, the coaches went out of their way to serve their athletes and make everyone feel included and cared for. Chuck Koeppen, whose combined boys' and girls' rosters regularly reached triple digits, cautioned that a coach "must be completely fair when dealing with both teams" in order for everyone to feel valued.

Everyone desires to live a meaningful life and "make a difference." In striving toward this life of meaning, the common wisdom of our age tends to be that you should seek direction by looking inward. Decide what your passions and values are, what you want from life, how you are gifted. But we have found in these coaches an echo of a more old-fashioned, practical, outward-looking method. Sure, these coaches evaluate their gifts and passions. But they seem to put more weight on the idea of service. Instead of "what do I want from life?" they seem to ask, "What does life want from me?"—an approach David Brooks points out in his bestselling book *The Road to Character (2015)*. Brooks suggests that meaningful lives begin with these questions: "What does this environment need in order to be made whole? What is it that needs repair? What tasks are lying around waiting to be performed?" (p. 22). These outward-looking questions capture the practical, service-oriented attitude of the coaches we interviewed.

Serving for the Greater Good

We hope young coaches will ask this question too: "What does this team of runners, and the greater running community, need from me?" The specific needs will change over time. Throughout our coaches' careers, the high school athletic experience has evolved and encountered new challenges along with many improvements. Technology gave us instant access to results and democratized the spread of training information. Small weekday meets against crosstown rivals have become nearly extinct as coaches have limited racing to large weekend invitationals to allow for more specified training during the week. This spread of information to parents and athletes has sometimes made them less trusting of their own coaches' expertise. Rick Weinheimer notices that athletes today seem more likely to ask, "Why?" But he doesn't see this as a bad thing because "it forces me to be sure to have a good reason for everything we do." A new generation of coaches likely will live squarely in the tension between the nostalgic image of sports as a fun learning experience and the demanding, competitive world of youth athletic specialization.

The sharing of results, live race webcasts, and statewide internet message forums have enabled this

specialization, but technology has also fostered a sense of community among teams across Indiana. This greater connectivity has improved practical learning and strengthened understanding among teams who now know much more about their opponents than ever before. As Chuck Koeppen pointed out, "Coaching across the state just keeps getting better and better." Koeppen's optimism stems from the measurable improvements Indiana keeps making as one of the nation's most competitive states in high school distance running. But Koeppen's confidence in the future also hints at an understanding that the most important things in our sport haven't changed at all. All our coaches find kids to be as receptive as ever to their messages of respect, gratitude, and positivity. What matters—"faith, family, academics, and athletics, in that order," according to Erhard Bell—hasn't changed. Kids still want to have fun and work hard. Cross country and track still function largely as a life learning experience, helping kids to grow and mature in their personal lives.

Nestled in our coaches' words about hard work and relentless self-improvement was a language of unfailing optimism toward their athletes. Words like *compassion* and *genuine care* and even *love*. First Corinthians, in the Bible, says that love believes the best about people, and these coaches have believed relentlessly in the potential of their runners. You know all those clichéd sports-movie moments when ragtag team members selflessly unite and overcome, under the guidance of a coach who is flawed yet pure of heart? Maybe Hollywood exaggerates the story sometimes, but those moments are rooted in an experience that is real for a lot of people. These great coaches consistently seek to serve others, lead by example, and care for every athlete. Those qualities transcend generational differences, and they will continue to shape the future of high school distance running in Indiana.

Enduring Wisdom

Appendix A: Won and Done

The following is the original text of the article from which this book was conceived. Since its publication in June 2016, Coach Weinheimer has retired.

WON AND DONE: The Exodus of State-Winning Boys Cross Country Coaches
By Derek Leininger

Over the past 20 years there have been 12 different head coaches whose teams have won the IHSAA boys cross country team state title: Colin Altevogt, Steve Lewark, Erhard Bell, Rick Weinheimer, Chuck Koeppen, Robert Seymour, Joe Brooks, Josh Fletcher, Doug Drenth, Michael Prow, Bill Wilke, and Eric Kellison.

Trivia Time ... of those 12, how many do you think are still active high school head boys cross country coaches in Indiana?

Answer: Two – Altevogt and Weinheimer

In fact, there are only three coaches who meet the following two criteria: 1) Head coach of a boys team state champion in cross country -and- 2) Still an active high school head boys cross country coach in Indiana:
Colin Altevogt, Carmel HS (2015 state champs)
Rick Weinheimer, Columbus North HS (2002, 2003, 2009, 2010, 2011 state champs)
Charles Warthan, Bloomington North HS (1980 state champs)

Over the past decade there has an exodus of some of the all-time great coaches in Indiana history. The coaching landscape has changed incredibly in a short

167

period of time. When I was a young coach, I contacted coaches who I thought were some of the best in the business. Over a period of several years I drove across the state to meet with each of them: Chuck Koeppen, Rick Weinheimer, Josh Fletcher, Mike Prow and Eric Kellison (to name a few) to pick their brains and ask them questions about training, coaching and leadership within their own programs. The only one of those coaches who is still a head boys coach in Indiana is Weinheimer.

In preparing for this story, I contacted Coach Weinheimer and asked him to reflect a little bit about the changes he has seen in his 38 years of coaching. He talked about when he first began: "I was in awe of my contemporaries ... Marshall Goss, Ralph Sieboldt, Charlie Warthan, Chuck Koeppen, Sam Rasmussen, Cabot Holmes, Bill Walker, Dick Conway, Tom Hathaway, Steve McIntyre. I was also fortunate to attend clinics and hear about coaching from the big names: Bill Dellinger, Arthur Lydiard, Peter Coe, Joe Vigil, and Joe Newton." Of those high school coaches, Warthan is the only one who is still coaching at the high school level.

So to quote Paula Cole circa 1997 ... Where Have All the Cowboys Gone? Of the 12 coaches listed above, here are the 10 who are no longer boys head coaches in Indiana and what they are doing now.

RETIREMENTS

Steve Lewark is the most recent retiree from our list. Lewark is riding off into the sunset with a trio of 4×800 state titles and a team cross country state title coming in his final two years coaching at West Lafayette HS.

Bill Wilke was a multi-generational staple at Portage HS in the 1970s, 80s and 90s. Wilke retired shortly after his fourth state title in 1999.

Joe Brooks won a pair of state titles with Warren Central in 2005 and 2006. Shortly after that De'Sean Turner-led group graduated, Brooks retired (as did WC track coach Dennis McNulty).

DIFFERENT SCHOOLS, DIFFERENT ROLES

Josh Fletcher won the 2004 state title as the boys coach at his own alma mater, Northridge HS. A few years ago Fletcher made the move to Penn HS and now coaches just girls track & field.

Erhard Bell won a pair of state titles with Carmel in 2012 and 2013, he is now an assistant coach with the Southport staff.

COACHING IN ANOTHER STATE

Michael Prow won a pair of state titles with Valparaiso HS 1997 and 2000. Two years ago he moved to Arizona and is currently teaching and coaching in a far warmer climate.

Doug Drenth won the 2001 state title with the outstanding Warrenburg, Riessen, Powers trio. After that year, he moved to Michigan and the last I heard he was coaching at a high school up there.

COACHING AT THE COLLEGE LEVEL

Chuck Koeppen is the most decorated coach in Indiana history, winning 11 boys state titles at Carmel. Koeppen now leads a resurgent mens cross country program at IUPUI.

MOVED INTO SCHOOL ADMINISTRATION

Robert Seymour led Fishers HS to the 2007 state title. You can still find Seymour at Fishers, but now he is a school administrator within the athletic department.

Eric Kellison led Franklin Central to the 1998 state title. Kellison retired from coaching a few years ago and is currently an Assistant Principal at Franklin Central HS.

Each of these coaches made the decision that was best for them and none of these decisions were connected. But when you look at this list, you can't help but realize just how many legendary coaches have left our sport in recent years.

LOOKING AHEAD

The story is the same when you look at the girls cross country coaches. There are only three state-winning girls head coaches who are still active high school coaches: Mark Ellington (Carmel HS), Rick Weinheimer (Columbus North HS) and Scott Lidskin (Westfield HS).

So it leads to the inevitable question ... who will be the next generation of legendary coaches? Who are the coaches currently in their 20s and 30s who will lead powerhouse programs in the years to come? Will coaches from the "millennial" generation stick around and coach at the same high school for 30+ years like so many of the "baby boomer" coaches did? It will be interesting to watch how the Indiana cross country coaching landscape continues to change in years to come.

APPENDIX B: IR REPORT- PAAVO DISTANCE TRAINING

A Closer Look at PAAVO Training (Part 1)
By Derek Leininger

If you were to survey coaches across Indiana and ask the question "What is the most highly criticized training program in Indiana high school cross country?" the answer would likely be PAAVO. For a number of reasons, this particular approach to distance training is polarizing: you are either for it or against it, very few people remain neutral.

Despite all the critics, the results are strong: six of the past seven team state titles in boys cross country have been won by PAAVO-trained teams (under 3 different head coaches). Additionally, in the past 20 years of Indiana high school boys track and field there have been two athletes who have pulled off the state title double, winning both the 1600 and 3200 meter runs in the same year: both of them were PAAVO-trained athletes (Christian Wagner and Ben Veatch).

So why is PAAVO so highly criticized? That is the question I seek to explore in this article (Part 1). We will take a look at some of the most common criticisms against PAAVO and try to assess how much validity there is to each argument. Next week (in Part 2) I will try to outline what PAAVO actually is.

First, let me state that I am not a PAAVO apologist. I coached cross country and track for 13 years and I did not implement the PAAVO training program with my athletes. I have no ulterior agenda in writing this article. I do consider myself a good friend with a number of PAAVO coaches and I have often wondered why there is so much antagonism toward this particular approach. So my goal is to explore this topic a little deeper and present my findings in a way that allows our audience to make an informed judgment about PAAVO.

It seems the best approach for Part 1 is to look at each argument separately. I asked Colin Altevogt (head boys cross country coach, Carmel HS) and Rick Weinheimer (head boys/girls cross country coach, Columbus North HS): What are the most common arguments that you hear about PAAVO? I am going to outline those arguments below and then give my own brief analysis on the validity of each comment. I will try to remain as objective and fair as I can.

Argument #1: PAAVO runners are high mileage.

Analysis: Do some PAAVO runners do high mileage? Yes, that is certainly true. Before we go any further, let us first quantify the term high mileage so that we are on the same page. Let's say that girls running 45+ miles per week and boys running 60+ miles per week are doing high mileage. You may come up with different numbers to define this, but let's just start there. There are definitely PAAVO athletes and programs exceeding these mileage amounts, no question. On the flip side, there are a number of non-PAAVO athletes exceeding these numbers, as well. It's not like PAAVO is the only training approach where high school athletes are running this much.

One thing I do know about the PAAVO program is that no athletes BEGINS at high mileage – they work up to that amount over an extended period of time. PAAVO is actually designed so that you don't increase in mileage until you have shown proficiency at your current mileage level. Mileage is totally individualized within PAAVO. Ben Veatch is a great example. Veatch won 5 individual state titles at Carmel (2 in cross country, 3 in track) and he was only running around 40 miles per week his senior year. He certainly does not meet our definition of high mileage.

Argument #2: PAAVO runners don't do well in college.

Analysis: My first response to this statement: What evidence do you have to support this claim? Are you looking at a couple of individuals who did not continue to improve in college running and then generalizing that to be true of all PAAVO runners? I have heard this statement numerous times, in person and on the message boards but I have never read any evidence attached to it. I know of a lot of PAAVO athletes who had outstanding college careers, and I know of many who did not. That statement would also be true of non-PAAVO runners. I cannot see any evidence that PAAVO training in high school has any negative effect on an athlete's college career.

Additionally, the transition from high school to college running is very difficult for many athletes. There are so many factors that affect a runner's success in college (being away from home, academic workload, injuries, personal motivation, different coaching style, different training approach, sleeping and eating habits, the college team culture, etc.). To attribute a lack of college success solely to an athlete's high school training doesn't make a lot of sense.

Argument #3: PAAVO runners run hard every day.

Analysis: This statement is just not accurate. PAAVO has recovery days built into their training program, just like every other training program. It is possible that some PAAVO programs run their recovery runs at a faster pace than other teams, but that does not mean that every day is a hard workout.

Argument #4: PAAVO runners get burnt out by the end of the season.

Analysis: State Meet results over the past several years would strongly suggest otherwise. Anecdotally, I would say the opposite is true: I find that PAAVO teams and athletes tend to hold up better later in the season than some non-PAAVO teams and athletes.

Argument #5: PAAVO is a secret society.

Analysis: This argument actually does have a lot of truth to it. PAAVO *seems* like a secret society because there is no book to buy about it. You would really have to sit down with a PAAVO coach or attend a PAAVO coaching clinic to learn more about PAAVO – and that is not always practical for people. If you do an Internet search for PAAVO training, the best thing you are likely to come up with are message board threads or short articles on running web sites that give you a very incomplete view of PAAVO. This "secret society" sense is something I will to try elucidate in Part 2 of this article.

Argument #6: PAAVO does not follow all of the best practices of physiology in distance training.

Analysis: In my opinion, there is some truth here. When you look at college and professional coaches, I don't know of any major programs or training groups that use the PAAVO training approach. If you believe that major college and professional coaches have a deep knowledge of physiology (as it applies to distance training), then the fact that they don't use PAAVO does give some credence to this argument. This, however, does not mean that PAAVO is void of sound physiology.

Argument #7: PAAVO training is too complicated.

Analysis: It is actually seems to be a pretty straightforward framework of training, once you take the time to understand it and have someone really explain it to you. Again, this is something that I hope to address more in Part 2 of this article.

Argument #8: PAAVO runners always get hurt.

Analysis: Much like the second argument, I find this argument hard to quantify. Do PAAVO runners get hurt? Sure they do. The problem with this argument is that I don't know any serious runner who has not dealt with injuries at some point in their career. When athletes (under any training program) push the limits of their bodies in training, injuries are bound to occur at some point. Do PAAVO runners get hurt more than other runners? I don't have any evidence to support or refute this claim.

In looking at the previous arguments, I tried to give brief and impartial analysis. Some of these arguments do have some truth to them, some of them are just factually inaccurate. Now that we have taken a brief look at some of the arguments against PAAVO, in Part 2 we will outline what PAAVO training actually looks like with the help of Columbus North Head Coach Rick Weinheimer and Carmel Head Coach Colin Altevogt.

A Closer Look at PAAVO Training (Part 2)

By Derek Leininger

Now that we have spent some time in Part 1 addressing some of the criticisms and misconceptions of Paavo, I will now attempt to clearly and concisely explain what Paavo actually is. I am going to use a Q & A format to try to accomplish this.

On a personal level, I consider Carmel boys coach Colin Altevogt and Columbus North boys/girls coach Rick Weinheimer to both be good friends of mine. I have spent countless hours talking to each of them about coaching, training and leadership. I have learned a great deal from them over the years. What I present below is my understanding of Paavo, based on the conversations that I have had with these two state championship cross country coaches.

Disclaimer: I am trying to explain Paavo as best as I can within the limitation of 1500 words. In order to properly implement any training program, you should have a comprehensive understanding of what workouts you are doing and when/why you are doing them. You should not expect to just copy and paste the Xs and Os of a training program and magically replicate the same results. Weinheimer said, "In my mind the two biggest keys to being successful with Paavo training are: 1. You must constantly teach the philosophy behind it. 2 As a coach you must believe in the importance of runners doing the right things on their own, independent of the coach." You cannot do either of those things unless you fully understand the purpose and structure of your training. I would argue that this is true of any training program, not just Paavo.

Okay, now let's jump into the Q & A format!

176

Q: What is the basic structure of Paavo training?

Here is the basic structure during the summer and winter training (what most people would call a "base phase" of running):

Monday – Long run (longest continual run of the week)
Tuesday – Short PPM (a hard run, 1-4 miles in length)
Wednesday – CT Run (basically a recovery run, different teams have different terms for this)
Thursday – Long PPM (a hard run, 2-10 miles in length, the heart of the Paavo program)
Friday – CT Run
Saturday – Longest Day (highest mileage day, broken into multiple runs, sometimes with a timed mile)
Sunday – CT Run (often the lowest mileage day of the week)

Notes:
PPM = Pace Per Mile
CT = Critical Threshold

Q: Can you adjust this structure at all?

Absolutely, coaches will make their own modifications. While this may be Paavo in its purest form, both Weinheimer and Altevogt said they make adjustments depending on the athlete's age and time of the year.

For example: Columbus North typically has freshmen do only one PPM per week. Carmel starts with a long PPM as the sole workout of the week and adds in the short PPM later in the summer. Carmel sometimes substitutes longer intervals on grass with short recovery time for a short PPM in late July or August. An example might be 2-3 x 2000 meter repeats with four minutes in between (instead of 3-4 mile short PPM).

Neither program has freshmen do the "longest day" – instead opting to let younger runners build into that as they get older and have a better base. Altevogt stated, "To me, the heart of Paavo training is doing what is best for the individual. This can be challenging for us since we have well over a hundred boys on our team, but we strive to find what is best for each person."

Q: What exactly is a PPM workout?

It is probably similar to what most people would call a tempo run. The PPM stands for pace per mile, and the goal of these workouts is to get the pace per mile faster while gradually increasing the distance. These are the hard workout days.

Q: What is the difference between a PPM and a typical tempo run?

It could be the intensity. While many coaches might give their runners a pace range or instructions to run "comfortably hard", a PPM is basically exerting a maximum effort over the course of that distance. The distance may be longer as well, building up to further distances over the course of four years than most other high school teams usually do.

Carmel runners typically max out at eight miles for a long PPM (not including warm-up and cool down) while Columbus North occasionally has boys go as far as ten miles. Columbus North girls usually build up to seven miles. Altevogt said, "For a PPM, we just tell our guys to do the best that they can. I think if you call it 'all-out' that people think they're supposed to sprint the whole way. Obviously that's not physically possible."

Q: Are there intervals in Paavo?

Yes. After the base phase, Paavo does transition into intervals in the fall season. These are often sessions of repeat 400s with a 400 meter jog recovery – so you

never stop moving. These intervals are run at a prescribed pace and reported in relation to that goal time. For example, if a runner's goal time was 75 seconds for 400 meters and he or she ran 72 seconds, the reported time would be "minus three" or "three under." If he or she ran 78 seconds, the report would be "plus three" or "three over." The objective is to run them at the target time with a quick rest pace. The goal time is created by a formula based on the pace of the best PPM at the farthest distance, and the number of intervals is based on the farthest distance. Like many other training methods, there are conversion tables to give paces for the 400s based on PPM performance.

These interval workouts are known interchangeably as continuous intervals (or CIs) and slow intervals (or SIs). There are two varieties of this workout: the low set and the high set. The number of intervals in the high set is half the volume of the long PPM so a 6-mile PPM would be 12×400 as a high set. The low set is four less than the high set.

In between intervals, athletes do a jog recovery, starting at around three minutes. The goal time stays the same but athletes try to run a faster jog and take less time in between intervals. The low set is typically used to shorten the rest time or speed up the rest jog while the high set matches that while adding volume.

Altevogt stated about the CI workouts: "They are essentially controlled chaos. It takes a lot of organization and meticulous planning at the start, but it is possible to get a pretty individualized workout for every kid on the team."

Q: I have heard that Paavo athletes run every day. Is that true?

Yes, one of the goals of Paavo training is to accumulate Consecutive Days (CDs). The basic premise is that every day is an opportunity to improve your oxygen delivery system and to recruit more capillaries. While this is one of the Paavo concepts, we have heard that Ben Veatch would cross train a few days each week – so again, individual modifications are made within Paavo.

Q: I am really interested in learning more about Paavo training. What can I do to learn more?

First, Weinheimer and Altevogt have both spoken at coaching clinics in the past and have outlined the Paavo training program in more detail. Here are a few links you could check out:

http://www.iatccc.org/notes/2011/weinheimer1.pdf

http://www.iatccc.org/notes/2011/weinheimer2.pdf

http://indianarunner.proboards.com/attachment/download/717

Those speech notes will give you some more information. My real suggestion would be to attend a

Paavo coaching clinic. For the past three winters (Jan/Feb) Fremont XC coach Moses Castillo has been hosting a Paavo clinic up at Fremont High School. Here is a link to last year's clinic information: http://paavo.us/coaching-clinics/indiana-seminar-2016/ That is where you will really learn to understand the "why" and be able to teach the philosophy of Paavo to your athletes, like Weinheimer said was vital to success.

Conclusion:
My goal with this two-part article was not to convert people to Paavo. My goal was to give factual information and to clear up misconceptions. My real hope is that coaches and athletes can use this information to improve.

I already stated in Part 1 that as a coach for 13 years I never implemented Paavo training with my athletes ... but I absolutely listened to what Weinheimer and Altevogt said and then I figured out how to incorporate some of the philosophies and ideas into my coaching. For example: over my last five years coaching at Snider HS we increased the length of our tempo runs with our older athletes – we challenged them to learn how to hold 30-40 minute hard tempo efforts (up to 7 miles) instead of the more typical 20 minutes (3-4 miles) that most training books adhere to. I could clearly see how successful the long PPMs were for the Columbus North and Carmel athletes in cross country, so I figured out how to take their ideas and apply them to my own practice. And our athletes were better for it. My hope is that this information will help other coaches learn something new that will benefit their athletes, as well.

Appendix C: Training Book Recommendations

Our coaches are a studious bunch, so we asked them to share some of the training books that they have found most helpful in their own learning and development as cross country coaches. Below is a list of the books that our coaches recommended, each listed by the number of coaches who mentioned that book. Any book recommended by at least two different coaches is included in the list below.

Recommendations, Title, Author

6 ... *Daniels' Running Formula*, Dr. Jack Daniels

5 ... *Run Run Run*, Fred Wilt

5 ... *Running to the Top*, Arthur Lydiard

5 ... *The Long Green Line*, Joe Newton and Karl Schindl

4 ... *Road to the Top*, Joe Vigil

4 ... *Running with the Buffaloes*, Chris Lear

3 ... *Coaching Cross Country Successfully*, Joe Newton and Joe Henderson

3 ... *How They Train*, Fred Wilt

3 ... *Lore of Running*, Tim Noakes

3 ... *The Complete Book of Running*, James Fixx

2 ... *Better Training for Distance Runners*, Dr. David Martin and Peter Coe

2 ... *Bowerman and the Men of Oregon*, Kenny Moore

2 ... *Galloway's Book on Running*, Jeff Galloway

2 ... *Once a Runner*, John L. Parker, Jr.

2 ... *Run with the Champions*, Marc Bloom

2 ... *Running Tough*, Michael Sandrock

2 ... *Running with the Legends*, Michael Sandrock

2 ... *Take the Lead*, Scott Simmons and Will Freeman

Enduring Wisdom

References

Brooks, D. (2015). *The road to character*. New York, NY: Random House.

Bronson, P. & Merryman, A. (2013). *Top dog: The science of winning and losing*. New York, NY: Hachette Book Group.

Covey, S. (1989). *The seven habits of highly effective people*. New York, NY: Simon & Schuster.

Daniels, J. (2005). *Daniels' running formula (2nd ed.)*. Champaign, IL: Human Kinetics. (Original work published in 1998)

Dubner, S. (2016, May 1). Being Malcolm Gladwell. *Freakonomics Radio Podcast*. Podcast retrieved from http://freakonomics.com/podcast/malcolm-gladwell/

Dudley, G.A., Abraham, W.M., & Terjung, R. L. (1982). Influence of exercise intensity and duration on biochemical adaptations in skeletal muscle. *Journal of Applied Physiology, 53* (4), 844-850. http://jap.physiology.org/content/53/4/844

Durkheim, E. (2001). *The elementary forms of religious life*. (C. Cosman trans.). Oxford: Oxford University Press. (Original work published 1912)

Dweck, C. (2006). *Mindset: The new psychology of success*. New York: Random House.

Dweck, C. (2006). *Test your mindset*. Retrieved from http://mindsetonline.com/testyourmindset/step1.php

Ericsson, K. A., Krampe, R. T., & Tesch-Römer, C. (1993). The role of deliberate practice in the acquisition of expert performance. *Psychological Review*, 100 (3), 363-406. Retrieved from http://projects.ict.usc.edu/itw/gel/EricssonDeliberatePracticePR93.PDF

Enduring Wisdom

Free Personality Test. (2011). Retrieved from
https://www.16personalities.com.

Gladwell, M. (2008). *Outliers: The story of success.* New York, NY:
Little, Brown and Company.

Goins, J. (n.d.). *Your mistakes don't define you, they teach you*
[Web blog post]. Retrieved January 10, 2017, from
https://goinswriter.com/mistakes-dont-define/

Granovetter, M. (1973). The strength of weak ties. *American
Journal of Sociology*, 78(6), 1360-1380.

Grant, A., Gino, F., & Hoffmann, D. (2010). The hidden
advantages of quiet bosses. *Harvard Business Review*.
Retrieved from https://hbr.org/2010/12/the-hidden-
advantages-of-quiet-bosses.
Grant, A. (2014). 5 myths about introverts and extroverts at work.
Government Executive. Retrieved from
https://www2.usgs.gov/humancapital/ecd/mentoringread
inglist/5MythsAboutIntrovertsandExtrovertsatWork.pdf.

Leonard, D. & Swap, W. (2005). *Deep smarts.* Boston, MA: Harvard
Business School Publishing Corporation.

McMillan, G. (2016). McMillan Running Calculator. Retrieved from
https://www.mcmillanrunning.com/

Muir, W. & Wilson, D. (2016). When the strong outbreed the weak:
an interview with william muir. *The Evolution Institute*.
Retrieved from https://evolution-
institute.org/article/when-the-strong-outbreed-the-weak-
an-interview-with-william-muir/

National Geographic News. (2007, April 2). Tsunami facts: How
they form, warning signs, and safety tips. *National
Geographic News*. Retrieved from
http://news.nationalgeographic.com/news/2007/04/0704
02-tsunami.html

Parker, J. (2010). *Once a runner: A novel*. New York, NY: Scribner.
(Original work published in 1978)

Pink, D. (2009). *Drive: The surprising truth about what motivates us*. New York, NY: Riverhead Books.

Praszkier, R. & Nowak, A. (2001). *Social entrepreneurship*. Cambridge: Cambridge University Press.

Reeve, J. (2009). Why teachers adopt a controlling motivating style toward students and how they can become more autonomy supportive. *Educational Psychologist*, 44(3), 159-175. Retrieved from http://johnmarshallreeve.org/yahoo_site_admin1/assets/docs/Reeve2009.3110625.pdf

Schmerling, R. H. (2015, Dec. 3). The gender gap in sports injuries. *Harvard Health Blog*. Retrieved from http://www.health.harvard.edu/blog/the-gender-gap-in-sports-injuries-201512038708

Science Learning Hub. (2011, May 2). *Shoaling*. Retrieved from https://www.sciencelearn.org.nz/resources/596-shoaling

Simmons, S. & Freeman, W. (2006). *Take the Lead*. Unknown publisher.

Weinheimer, R. (2015). *Move your chair*. CreateSpace Independent Publishing.

Made in the USA
Columbia, SC
22 December 2020